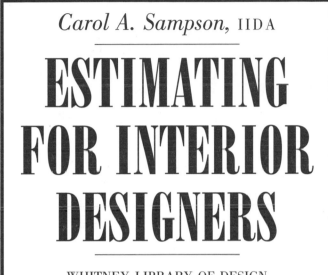

Carol A. Sampson, IIDA

ESTIMATING FOR INTERIOR DESIGNERS

WHITNEY LIBRARY OF DESIGN
an imprint of Watson-Guptill Publications/New York

Photo Credits. Page 8: Photographer–Lydia Cutter. Designer–Janelle Schick, ASID. Page 10: Photographer–John Harding Dey, ASID. Page 12: Photographer–A.F. Payne Photography. Designer–Janelle Schick, ASID. Page 14: Photographer–Mark Palmer Photography. Designer–Carol Sampson, IIDA. Page 28: Photographer–Michael Perham. Designer–Carol Sampson, IIDA. Page 31: Photographer–Mark Boisclair Photography. Designer–Janelle Schick, ASID. Page 33: Designer–Janelle Schick. Pages 48, 80, 176: Photographer–Dino Tonn Photography. Designer–Janelle Schick. Pages 79, 185: Photographer–John Mate Photography. Designer–Kim McClain, Assoc. IIDA, Allied ASID. Page 116: Designer–George Taack, IIDA. Page 143: Photographer–Mark Palmer. Designer: Carol Sampson, IIDA. Page 146: Photographer–John Mate. Designer: Connie Humphrey, IIDA & Kim McClain. Pages 156, 169: Photographer–Scott Sandler Photography. Designer: Feathers Interiors. Page 180: Designer–Janice Schick. Page 183: Photographer–Mark Boisclair Photography. Designer–Janelle Schick. Page 185: Photographer—John Mate. Designer—Kim McClain. Page 194: Photographer–Harold Davis Photography. Designer–Carol Sampson.

Edited by Elizabeth Wright.
Designed by Bob Fille, Graphiti Design, Inc..
Production Manager: Hector Campbell.
Text set in Boboni Book.

First edition pubished in 1991 and revised edition published in 2001 by Watson-Guptill Publications, a division of VNU Business Media, Inc., 770 Broadway, New York, NY 10003
www.watsonguptill.com

Library of Congress Control Number and Data: 2001089128

ISBN 0-8230-1629-3

Printed in the U.S.A.

First printing, 2001

4 5 6 7 8 9 / 08 07 06 05 04 03

Acknowledgments

This is a book of estimating procedures covering various materials, costs and time tables for eight different trades; painting, wall covering, hard flooring, carpet, window treatments, bed coverings, tablecloths, and upholstery. There were previously no books or reference materials combining these estimating subjects into one easily available source for interior designers.

After accumulating the information over many years as a designer and storing it in several different locations around my office but never being able to put my hands on it without a lengthy search, I decided to combine my data and write a book on estimating. I further researched the techniques and developed many formulas and charts that would reflect an industry wide application. Designers, workrooms and trades people would all be able to communicate more accurately using the same information.

I was able to fine tune and test out the materials and formulas used to write this book while teaching courses at San Bernardino Valley College and at University of Cal at Riverside (UCR) over a five year period of time. This book is a teaching tool for the new students of interior design.

I would like to thank all those who patiently helped me with information, advice and those who proofread my results; including many installers, workrooms, upholstery shops, tradespeople and subcontractors. A special thanks to Lynn Korzelus who gave me the opportunity to teach estimating. Thanks to Henry Starns who answered my endless questions on painting. Many thanks to Cheryl Ghormley for months of computer work and to Patricia Brock for her drawings and illustrations. Much thanks to Norma Pou for helping me find a publisher and deep gratitude to Carol, Jim and Joshua for constant support and encouragement. I would also like to thank my son, John for preparing many dinners and aiding me with his computer skills.

Contents

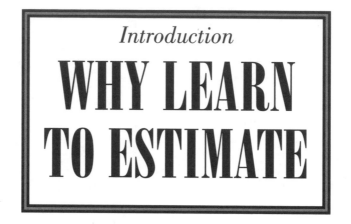

WHY LEARN TO ESTIMATE

The ability to create accurate estimates for materials, costs, and time is critical for interior designers when working on either residential or commercial projects. Estimating the materials and labor properly is both a challenge and a problem-solving situation, but it need not be a difficult or time-consuming task. There are formulas, short cuts, and charts that cut down on time required to estimate while giving you reliable figures. Strong estimating skills will enable you to work better with clients, prepare accurate, comprehensive estimates, figure accurate completion dates, and verify subcontractors' figures.

WORKING WITH CLIENTS

Every design project requires the compilation of various figures, specifications, and labor costs in order to present to the client an accurate and detailed idea of the project costs. The ability to estimate will allow you to adapt various design concepts to the client's budget, as well as adjust or change the project budget while the client is present. There are thousand-dollar jobs along with the million-dollar jobs-good design has no set price. Any design budget can be reduced or increased, depending on the client's needs and preferences.

Many residential, as well as commercial, clients have an idea of the amount they want to spend. However, they often find the fabrics, carpets, or furniture pieces they have chosen are more expensive than they had anticipated. If certain parts of the design concept are over their budget they will want to know how to preserve the look they seek without the extra costs. Reestimating with different materials is the logical answer.

Accurate estimating is important for any project. An estimate that is too high can prevent the designer from getting the interior design project in the first place. If, on the other hand, the estimate is too low, the designer stands an excellent chance of getting the project, but no chance at all of making a profit-the designer may even lose money because of overlooked expenses. There are stories of designers who have gone out of business because they "ate the job" because of "hidden" costs not estimated that the designer was obligated to pick up. If the designer does not know how to estimate he or she has to rely on a person from the workroom to put together the estimate who may not really understand the designer's concepts and give inaccurate figures.

ACCURATE COMPLETION DATES

The "time is money" quote is no different for the interior design project. Commercial projects especially will need to have a completion date deadline. The company will need to plan in advance for moving and installing other equipment that is not part of the design project, such as audio visual equipment, files, stock items, and so forth. They will also need to move, hire, or let go personnel. All the employees and executives need to know when they can move into their new spaces. The interior design must be completed on time so that the move affecting many people can be executed.

VERIFY SUBCONTRACTOR'S FIGURES

Perhaps one of the most important reasons for a designer to know how to estimate is to verify the subcontractor's figures. An out-of-line estimate can alert the designer to an incompetent subcontractor or an inexperienced worker. In addition, the designer that is ignorant of estimating cannot be alerted to the supplier or installer that takes advantage of the situation. Many stories fill the trade about extra wallpaper or carpet that found its way into someone else's house at the designer's and client's expense.

Intelligent comparisons can be made between various bidders for the work, based on a set standard of estimates specified. The designer's professional ability to determine the quality of work called for, the type of labor required, and the materials and equipment necessary to meet the job specifications are essential on every design project.

Seven coats of faux painting using wall texture, powdered bronze, several colors, and a finish glaze.

P eople have been decorating walls with paint for over 5,000 years. The first documented wall paintings were the Lascaux, France cave paintings dated between 15,000 to 10,000 B.C. However, these are believed to have been used for religious ceremonial rituals rather than purely decorative purposes. Decorative painting as we know it today was first used by the ancient Egyptians and the process they used 5,000 years ago is nearly the same as the one used today. Before painting a tomb mural, the stone was covered with plaster. After the plaster had cured or dried, the paint was applied, followed by a protective clear coat of varnish or wax. The early Egyptians favored geometric patterns using plant-like designs such as the papyrus and lotus. Some of their mural themes were daily life, royal escapades, and funerary customs. Unique to their art and history was the practice of combining paint with wall carvings. Their colors have remained fresh over the centuries due to the use of minerals for the pigment or color, which are very similar to tempera paints used today. Their paint has carried through to present time using a simple mixture of pigment (color), water, and either wax or glue as the binder.

The excavation of the ash-preserved ruins of Pompeii enabled the world to see examples of the beautiful realistic painted wall art done by the ancient Greeks and Romans. The detail and the colors of the scenes were breathtaking. Painted architectural decorations adorned the rooms of every villa. There were scenes of gardens, animals, architectural buildings, and people—wealthy and poor—at work and play. Highlighting, shades, and shadows produced a trompe l'oeil relief effect of marbles, inlaid stones, and wood.

In the seventh century, while Europe was enduring the Middle Ages, China was developing decorative painting techniques. Rich lacquered walls are a Chinese hallmark covering many centuries of interiors. Over thirty years ago, the tomb of Princess Yung Tai was excavated. The ceilings and walls of the passageway and chamber were covered with colorful wall paintings, with scenes reflecting the princess's palace life with many female attendants painted in lifelike postures.

During the Renaissance, there was an explosion of wall mural painting done all over Europe in palaces, churches, chateaus, villas, and castles. Traveling aristocrats, who enjoyed this art form in foreign countries, brought the concepts back with them to duplicate in their own homes. The tradition of wall painting has continued through to today's interiors. Special paint techniques such as marbling, graining, and glazing have been in vogue for the last several centuries in Italy, France, England, and the United States.

Trompe l'oeil, (pronounced tromp loy), is a two-dimensional painting technique that has been used for thousands of years; it momentarily tricks the viewer into believing painted images are real three-dimensional objects or actual vistas-trompe l'oeil is French for "deceive the eye."

Trompe l'oeil can be traced back to the Greek and Roman periods, when huge, painted wall murals were popular in the homes of the very wealthy. Complicated,

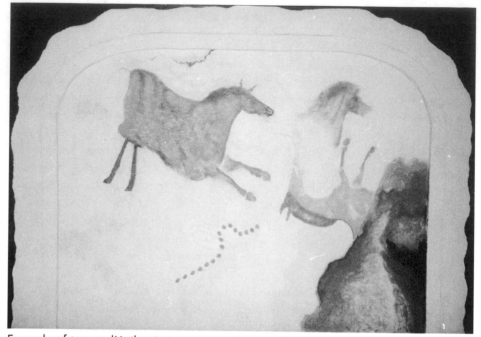

Example of trompe l'óeil painting; cave painting at Lascaux, France.

intricate landscapes and elaborate, interior architectural details were painted on most walls—some as high as thirty feet in aristocratic villas and palaces. In Tuscany, the Italian Palladio villas of the Renaissance period were painted with gorgeous, trompe l'oeil frescos by famous artists of the time; these villas are now open to the public for viewing.

Interior designers of the twenty-first century can use tromp l'oeil in many creative ways in any room—even on some furniture pieces. Some examples include: decorative area rugs painted on bare floors or fluffy clouds painted on ceilings. Plain entryways can be dressed up with painted marble columns or painted pulled-back velvet drapery trimmed in fringes and topped with elegant swags. Large, flat walls can be given architectural details by painting rows of cornices, moldings, chair rails, and baseboards. Painting in a few wall niches filled with classic statuary imparts sophistication to entryway and hallway walls. Dining room walls invite painted landscapes with balconies, trellises, foliage, birds and other small animals such as rabbits, cats, and dogs. Dull hallways can be cheered up using some imaginative tromp l'oeil techniques. At the turn-of-the-century, many homes featured trompe l'oeil flooring in their entryways rather than the expensive actual flooring—this is still an attractive option. Canvas is first painted to look like marble tiles or inlaid wood, then stretched and sealed with varnish. And of course, children's bedrooms can be the most fun to paint with all kinds of trompe l'oeil themes, fables, adventures, and characters.

The one room that gets by far the most trompe l'oeil painting in today's market is the kitchen. Here, whimsical combinations on a large or small scale can amuse and delight the viewer. Trompe l'oeil cabinets, hutches and shelves can appear to be spilling over with utensils, antiques, or baskets filled with fruits and vegetables. Fanciful windows with wood braces, drapery, flowerpots and scenery can be painted on blank walls. Painted garlands in either floral or fruit and vegetable combinations are a colorful way to complete these windows.

Many restaurants display trompe l'oeil paintings to create an interesting focal point in a room. Such artwork is easy to take down and clean or move to another location for variety.

Trompe l'oeil can be painted on properly prepared plaster walls, wood panels or canvas. Whether used as a way to make a small space seem bigger or as an amusing and entertaining conversation-piece in a room, trompe l'oeil is one of the interior designer's most versatile, delightful painting techniques. Pricing will vary widely depending on the intricacies of the painted design, how much time it will take to complete, and, most importantly, the expertise of the artist/painter.

Faux (pronounced fo) is a French word meaning "fake or false." When used to refer to paint finishes used on walls and furniture, faux means the creation of beautiful, aged-looking surfaces that mimic the look of marble, wood grain, leather, tortoise shell, stone, adobe or weathered bricks. Faux painting uses layers of colors, creating a textural effect and evoking an elegance reminiscent of European castles, palaces, churches, and villas. Contemporary styles of faux finishes combine layers of color with other textural elements such as metallic foil, straw, tissue-paper, or heavier paper. Textural effects can be added to the finish by combing with a trowel, adding pastes or powders, sponging multiple colors, spot-spraying, rubbing with a rag or scraper, and brush-splattering. Techniques vary with each artist/painter—leaving an endless variety of possibilities for the gorgeous final effects.

Faux finishes can be applied to columns, fireplaces, walls, and furniture; each layer of paint increases the depth and beauty of the finished surface. Faux-finish accents such as stencils and borders can be used around walls, windows, floors, and on furniture for a delightful whimsy or a much more serious historical restoration.

Sometimes four to eight layers of different colors will have to be applied to achieve the desired look; each coat needs plenty of time to dry before the next is applied. When the final layer is dry, a final finish-coat of wax, varnish or glaze must be applied to preserve all the colors and protect all the careful work underneath. Faux finishes are complex and sophisticated, but they are also time-consuming and labor-intensive. They create a uniquely custom-made appearance. These finishes, or any kind of historical preservation, require the expertise of professional craftspeople.

Painting is the most essential, dramatic design tool available to designers. Most design projects will require the use of subtle or historical paint colors for wall sur-

Faux ceiling paint and a stencil accent.

faces, trims, furniture, and a multitude of decorative treatments. Paint can be the least expensive tool a designer uses, yet it can be the one that makes the greatest difference in a room.

PAINT BASICS

The subjects of paint and painting can be very complex and can take many years to master. The information here, while simplified, is suitable for estimating most interior design projects. For complex projects, various other professional sources can provide detailed, expert information.

Paint Materials. All paints comprise of three parts: a base, a pigment, and a binder or vehicle. The base is what gives the paint its covering quality. White lead was originally used as a paint base until the discovery of its high toxicity. Today's base is made from synthetics—polyesters, polyurethane, and polyamide. Pigments give the paint its color and intensity and have an unlimited color range. Nine or ten different pigments sometimes can be added before the color starts to turn muddy. Many fine painting craftspeople mix their own paint colors. Light colored paints should be mixed slowly, adding small amounts of pigments to the mixture of the base and binder, and testing against the desired sample. When mixing dark paints, it is easier to begin with a premixed paint close to the desired color and then add other pigments until the correct color is achieved. The binder holds the base and the pigments together, and adheres the paint to surfaces. In interior paint, the binder can be linseed oil, varnish, glue, casein, or synthetics, each with a specific purpose.

There are two types of paint: solvent-based and water-based. Solvent-based paints are commonly oil- or synthetic-based. They are very durable, can be scrubbed repeatedly, and are highly resistant to stains and other damage. Enamel paints are considered solvent-based paints because their base is varnish or synthetic alkyd. The water-based paints are generally latex or synthetic. These paints are also very durable, long-lasting, and resistant to abrasions. The biggest advantages of water-based paints are that they are easy to apply, fast-drying, and easy to clean up.

All paints come in three types of finishes: flat, gloss, and semigloss. Interior paints have specific characteristics that are important for different interior surfaces. Flat finished paints are generally used for interior walls, excluding kitchens, bathrooms, laundry rooms, and playrooms, where heavy scrubbing and scuffing require a strong wall paint. Flat finishes reduce glare, but also show dirt faster, especially around light switches and doorways. High-gloss paints have a very shiny surface and are generally used on woodwork, doors, and sometimes on walls when a specific effect is desired. Often referred to as trim paints, high-gloss paints clean quickly and easily. The hard surfaces of these paints deflect dings and scratches. Semigloss paints have the positive characteristics of both flat and high-gloss paints. They are commonly used on baseboards, window and door trims, and the walls of kitchens, bathrooms, laundry rooms, nurseries, and playrooms.

"House paint" is the commercial term for exterior paints, which are generally applied to siding and other large, exterior wall spaces. Many house paints have extra added features formulated for a particular requirement such as a rust preventive for metal trim. House paints are available either solvent-based or water-based in the same finishes of flat, gloss, and semigloss.

When selecting a paint color from sample chips, it is best to choose a color two shades lighter than the shade desired. Colors look darker when covering a large area, and it is a common mistake to choose a color too dark, especially when looking at a tiny paint sample. In painting, the best results are gained from using fewer paint coats. Too many layers of paint can crack or peel. As a general rule, pastel colors need one primer coat and one paint coat. For darker colors, use one primer coat and two or three paint coats to completely cover walls. And keep in mind, when reversing from dark to light, two or three paint coats may be necessary to lighten walls.

Faux painted walls and border.

Special Painting Techniques. Special painting techniques have been in vogue for several thousand years. The many used in today's interiors are virtually unchanged and just as beautiful as they were in antiquity. They can be applied to any surface that will accept paint such as walls, ceilings, moldings, floors, and furniture. Marbling and graining techniques can achieve rich and unique marble and wood effects. Sponging, crackling, spattering, and combing are all different techniques used to create the illusion of texture. Stenciling is the use of a cut-out pattern over and over as in a border. Each technique requires different amounts of paint coats and different skill levels depending on the specific job. These techniques will need to be priced on a per job basis by the craftsperson because each job will be unique, since it will be designed and created specifically for the individual client's needs.

Painting Finishes. After all the paint coats have been properly applied, sometimes the painted surface needs to be protected by a finish coat. Finish coats can

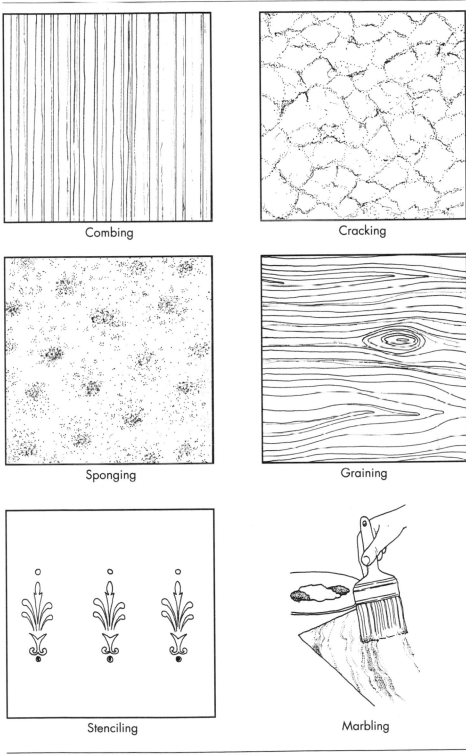

Combing

Cracking

Sponging

Graining

Stenciling

Marbling

be one of several products, depending on both the budget and the intended final appearance of the surface. The most common finish coats are varnishes, lacquers, shellacs, and glazes. When using a varnish, several coats need to be built up with lots of polishing or rubbing in between each coat. Varnishes will cast an old world brownish tone to the surface and will require renewing about every six months. Lacquers can be either transparent or opaque and are durable and tough with gloss, satin, or matte finishes. Shellac is the least durable finish coat. It has a soft, satiny finish that is very fragile and will not hold up to heat or moisture. Glaze is used often because it is a thin, watery coat of oil and turpentine with a small amount of color or pigment added. It will not turn brown, need polishing between coats, or require renewing like the other finish coats. Glazing is the preferred finish coat after walls have been painted, grained, marbled, sponged, or spattered.

Preparation of Surfaces. Preparation can be the most time-consuming and important phase of a painting project. Correctly done, it will ensure a beautiful, long-lasting job. Even the most expensive high-quality paint will not adhere well to an excessively dusty or greasy surface, nor will paint hide large cracks or holes. When working with a professional painter, let him or her know how far to take the preparation part of the job: minimal, average, or extensive. All surfaces that will receive paint should be smooth, clean, and dry. Kitchens absorb a film of cooking grease and grime that has to be removed for good paint adhesion. Bathrooms are exposed to shower steam, body oils, and sprays that cling to both walls and ceilings. All of these surfaces need cleaning with detergent solution, ammoniated cleansers, or mineral spirits. On older drywall and plaster surfaces, hairline cracks and chips need to be filled with spackling compound. Large cracks and holes need repair work with a special patching plaster. Areas around doors, windows, and baseboards need to be sealed with caulking before painting. After the patches have completely dried, the surface is sanded smooth and flush with the surrounding surface.

New walls of either drywall or plaster need special treatment. Drywall needs a coat of latex primer or paint to seal its paper surface. The second coat of paint can then be either a solvent-based or water-based paint in a flat, gloss, or semigloss finish. New plaster walls have to be thoroughly cured for about two months to allow moisture to escape as the plaster dries. If uncured plaster must be painted, apply one coat of water-based latex paint primer and then follow with other coats of latex paint. The latex paint will not affect the drying process so that the alkali in the new plaster will continue to allow moisture to evaporate from the walls. If you can wait two months for the plaster to cure, then you can use an oil-based or solvent-based paint both as a primer coat and for subsequent paint coats.

All surrounding surfaces must be protected before any patching or painting begins. Existing rooms that are being refurbished need more protection than new constructions. In existing commercial and residential spaces, flooring must be covered thoroughly with drop cloths or tarps to keep those surfaces from paint splatters. Window glass should be taped with paper. All outlets, switch plates, and heating and air conditioning registers need to be removed. And of course, any furniture in the area must be covered. Preparation can take several days to complete before the actual painting begins.

Job Grades. Paint jobs are classified by grade-minimum, standard, and premium—reflecting the difference in the quality and cost of the work. Be sure of the quality of work needed for each project and convey this to the painter. For example, commercial work would require a fast, minimal quality of workmanship. A basic residential wall painting could be of standard quality, while specialty painting such as lacquered walls would qualify for a premium job because there would be more paint needed and longer labor hours. Lacquered walls need to be rubbed and polished between each coat of lacquer and there could be three to fifteen coats used on a premium job.

ESTIMATING PAINT MATERIALS

Understanding basic painting estimating and costs helps to verify the subcontractor's figures and alerts the designer to an inexperienced or incompetent worker. An overly low estimate may indicate that certain expenses have been overlooked or that a procedure has been left out of the bid (such as a second or third coat of paint, or even the cleanup phase). On projects where there are several bids, you must be able to correctly analyze the submitted bids and make genuine comparisons.

There are two types of estimating for every job: by square feet and by linear feet.

Square Feet. Square-feet estimating applies to walls, doors, ceilings, trusses, cabinets, cornices, casework, floor surfaces, and totally exposed surfaces of radiators. Openings in the walls, such as windows, are usually not subtracted from the measurements because the extra time required to protect them offsets any savings in material or labor.

Square-feet estimating is done primarily for new construction where the amount of preparation is minimal. For painting done in remodeling or refurbishing, the estimating becomes closer to "guesstimating" because each job has so many variables that enter into the final estimate. Square-feet estimating is found by multiplying the length of a wall by its height. For example: four living room walls are all 12 feet wide and 8 feet high; 12' + 12' + 12' + 12' = 48' x 8' = 384 total square feet. Divide the number of square feet a gallon of paint will cover (see Paint/Labor Chart on page 20). This example would need about one gallon of paint for one coat since most gallons cover approximately 300 to 600 square feet. This amount will vary depending on the painter and the covering capacity of the paint over the texture of a given surface. Variables would include the condition of wall surfaces, the amount of preparation required, and the experience of the painter.

Paint/Labor Chart

Surface Type	Paint Type	First or Primer Coat	Finish or Consecutive Coats	Total No. of Coats (Including Primer Coat)	1-Gallon Coverage in Sq. Ft.	Brushwork	Roller	Spray
		PAINT				LABOR Hours per 100 Sq. Ft.		
Drywall (sheetrock)	Latex (water-based)	Latex		1	250-400 First coat	1 hour	30 min.	20 min.
			Flat	2-3	400-600			
			Semi-gloss	2-3	Consecutive			
			High-gloss	2-3	coats			
	Alkyd (solvent-based)	Latex		1	300-400 First coat	1 hour	30 min.	20 min.
			Flat	2-3	400-600			
			Semi-gloss	2-3	Consecutive			
			High-gloss	2-3	coats			
	Epoxy (solvent-based)	Enamel	Semi-gloss	2-4	400	1 hour	30 min.	20 min.
	Urethane (solvent-based) (with color)	Enamel	Semi-gloss	2-4	400	1 hour	30 min.	20 min.
	Varnish (solvent-based)	Enamel	Semi-gloss	2-3	550-650	1 hour	30 min.	20 min.
Plaster	Latex	Latex		1	400-600 First coat	1 hour	30 min.	20 min.
			Flat	2-3	300-500			
			Semi-gloss	2-3	Consecutive			
			High-gloss	2-3	coats			
	Alkyd	Alkyd or Latex		1	400-600 First coat	1 hour	30 min.	20 min.
			Flat	2-3	300-500			
			Semi-gloss	2-3	Consecutive			
			High-gloss	2-3	coats			
	Urethane (with color)	Enamel	Semi-gloss	2-4	400-600	1 hour	30 min.	20 min.
Wood-Flooring	Latex	Latex	Enamel	2-3	500-700	30 min.	20 min.	15 min.
	Alkyd	Alkyd	Enamel	2-3	500-700	30 min.	20 min.	15 min.
	Epoxy (with or without color)	Epoxy	Enamel	2-3	500-700	15 min.	10 min.	10 min.

PAINT

Paint/Labor Chart

Surface Type	Paint Type	First or Primer Coat	Finish or Consecutive Coats	Total No. of Coats (Including Primer Coat)	1-Gallon Coverage in Sq. Ft.	Brushwork	Roller	Spray
Wood Flooring	Lacquer	Lacquer	High-gloss	2-6	500-700	1 hour	10 min.	10 min.
	Stain (with pigment)	Wood Sealer	Semi-gloss	2-3	300-500	1 hour	10 min.	10 min.
	Shellac	Shellac	Semi-gloss	2-4	400-500	1 hour	10 min.	10 min.
	Wax	Wood Sealer	Semi-gloss	3-8	200-400	1 hour		
	Urethane (with color)	Urethane	High-gloss	2-4	500-700	1 hour 15 min.		
	Varnish	Wood Sealer	High-gloss	3-4	500-700	1 hour 15 min.		
Wood-Trim & Paneling	Latex	Enamel	Flat Semi-gloss High-gloss	2-3	300-600	30 min		15 min.
	Alkyd	Enamel	Flat Semi-gloss High-gloss	2-3	400-600	30 min.		15 min.
	Epoxy (with or without color)	Enamel Undercoat or Epoxy	High-gloss	2-4	400-600	20 min.		10 min.
	Lacquer	Lacquer	High-gloss	2-6	500-700	20 min.		10 min.
	Stain (with color)	Wood Sealer	Semi-gloss	2-3	200-500	20 min.		10 min.
	Shellac	Shellac	Semi-gloss	2-4	400-500	20 min.		10 min.
	Urethane (with color)	Enamel or Urethane	High-gloss	2-4	400-500	20 min.		10 min.
	Varnish	Wood Sealer	Semi-gloss High-gloss	3-4	400-600	20 min.		10 min.
Cabinets & Casework	Latex	Wood Sealer	Semi-gloss	3-4	400-600	20 min.		
	Epoxy (with color)	Epoxy	Semi-gloss High-gloss	2-4	300-600	20 min.		

Paint/Labor Chart

| | | PAINT | | | | LABOR Hours per 100 Sq. Ft. | | |
Surface Type	Paint Type	First or Primer Coat	Finish or Consecutive Coats	Total No. of Coats (Including Primer Coat)	1-Gallon Coverage in Sq. Ft.	Brushwork	Roller	Spray
Cabinets & Casework	Stain	Wood Sealer	Semi-gloss	2-4	300-500	20 min.		
	Shellac	Shellac	Semi-gloss	2-3	300-500	20 min.		
	Varnish	Wood Sealer	High-gloss	3-4	400-600	20 min.		
Doors	Latex	Latex	Semi-gloss High-gloss	3-4	300-600	1 hour 30 min.		
	Stain (with pigment)	Wood Sealer	Flat Semi-gloss	3-4	400-600	1 hour 30 min.		
Ceilings- Drywall or Plaster	Latex	Latex	Flat	2-3	300-600 (Acoustic 3 times)		45 min.	30 min.
	Alkyd	Alkyd	Flat	2-3	300-600		45 min.	30 min.
Paint Removal- Walls	Latex or Alkyd					2 hours		
	Lacquer					2 hours		
	Varnish					2 hours		
Trim	Latex or Alkyd	DONE ON TIME AND MATERIAL ONLY				1 hour 30 min.		
	Varnish					1 hour 30 min.		
	Lacquer	OR BY THE JOB				4 hours 30 min.		
Floors	Varnish					1 hour 15 min.		
	Wax					45 min.		
	Latex or Alkyd					1 hour 45 min.		
Doors	Varnish					1 hour 30 min.		

These times will vary widely according to the intricacies of the job and the amount of previous paint buildup.

Linear Feet. Linear-feet estimating is done for any painting done in a straight line or running foot. Linear-feet estimating applies to piping, interior trim around doors, baseboards, chair rails, crown moldings, and stair rail assemblies—including posts, rails, balusters by number of pieces for total length in feet. For example: the moldings on four living room walls are 12 feet long each; 12' + 12' + 12' + 12' = 48 linear feet. The linear feet then need to be converted back to square feet. Any object that is up to 3 inches wide is considered a quarter of a foot. In the example of moldings 48 linear feet long, if they are 3 inches wide you would use the following formula: 48 linear feet ÷ 4 = 12 square feet. Now this amount can be estimated according to the Paint/Labor Chart on page 20.

How to Use the Paint/Labor Chart. The first column of the painting chart lists the type of surface the paint will be covering: plaster, drywall, woodwork, and so forth. The second column lists the kind of paint needed for the wall surface; for example, drywall can be covered with latex or water-based paint. The third column lists the type of primer needed to seal the drywall surface. Any primer coat will use more paint as the raw surface will soak up paint like a sponge. The second coat or finish coat (fourth column) will have a look or texture to it such as flat, semigloss, or high-gloss. There can be anywhere from one finish coat on a plain wall to fifteen finish coats of lacquer for custom lacquered walls. The fifth column lists the total minimum amount of both primer and finish coats needed for the surface being painted. The sixth column lists the average amount of paint coverage in square feet for one gallon of paint. (For example, one gallon of primer will cover only 250 to 400 square feet of drywall because raw drywall is very absorbent. The next layer of paint has greater spread because one layer of primer has already been applied. Therefore, one gallon used for the second coat will now cover 400 to 600 square feet.) The seventh, eighth, and ninth columns list the labor time it would take to paint 100 square feet (one wall 12 feet wide, 8 feet high) using a brush, roller, or spray. Special painting techniques are not included on the chart because no basic standards are available due to the highly specialized nature of the work.

COST ESTIMATING

Five factors will affect cost estimating for paint: material costs, labor costs, equipment costs, overhead, and profit.

Material Costs. The materials needed to accomplish the painting project include (in addition to the paint in gallons, either premixed or mixed on the job) turpentine, varnish, shellac, putty, caulking, linseed oil, sandpaper, and other preparatory materials. Every job would require some of these materials, but not necessarily all of them. Some painters will charge for every item they use on the job; that is, every piece of sandpaper, every roll of masking tape, and so forth. Other painters will simply charge ten to fifteen dollars for miscellaneous consumable items related to each job.

Labor Costs. Painting labor costs are calculated on the time required to paint 100 square feet of a given surface. The time spent in preparation, actual painting, and cleanup are included in this figure. Preparation time will depend on the amount of preparation required for the particular job. Before the job begins, indicate to the painter the level of preparation required: minimal, average, or extensive (see Preparation of Surfaces on page 16). Labor time also includes the length of time it takes to do the actual painting. This time is determined by the efficiency of the workman and the intricacy of the job. Obviously, an experienced painter will not take as long as a newer, inexperienced person. Also, a design project using a special paint technique, such as glazing, which requires multiple coats of paint, will take more time than a basic two-coat paint project.

Scheduling can become an extra labor cost when the work takes place outside the standard, nine-to-five work week. When painting a commercial space would interfere with the workday activities, it is sometimes necessary to have the job done at night or on a weekend. This way the painters can spread out their equipment without interfering with the employees' activities.

Economic factors can also affect labor cost. If jobs are plentiful, prices will be higher. If jobs are scarce, prices will be lower. September through Christmas is the highest-priced season of the year because many people want their homes to look good for the holidays. Trade-union standards can also affect a commercial project where minimums in labor cost are usually higher.

Location of the project enters into the labor costs when there is scaffolding involved—when cathedral ceiling or two-story walls need to be painted. Special insurance may be needed for unique and potentially dangerous projects. Also, jobs based out of town will incur extra charges.

The final labor cost to factor in is the cleanup phase. This phase includes touching up missed spots, cleaning paint drops, scraping paint from glass surfaces, and any other general cleanup or detailing.

Equipment costs. The equipment needed for each job can be basic or complicated. The basics include brushes, rollers, hand tools, ladders, rags, buckets, scrapers, and drop cloths. For a more involved painting project, special equipment may be needed, such as sprayers, scaffolding, sponges, combs, and stencils. Special equipment will increase the job costs.

Overhead. The overhead for the painter includes business expenses, such as rent, phone, insurance, truck maintenance, and gasoline, items not chargeable to any particular part of the work. Overhead costs are calculated at 10 to 15 percent of the sum of labor and materials. On the sum of labor alone, overhead may run from 15 to 20 percent.

Profit. Profit is calculated at 10 to 15 percent of the sum of the total costs of labor, materials, equipment, and overhead for the specific job.

TIME ESTIMATING

Scheduling painting projects and determining the amount of time required to accomplish each job will be different for each client. Working closely with the paint contractor will help to gain experience in estimating time more clearly. And using the labor section of the Paint/Labor Chart on page 20 will provide somewhat of a guide to estimating time for a project.

The main determining factor in estimating time will be the amount of preparation required. New construction of a custom-designed home or a commercial building needs little preparation because the painter does not have to work around carpeting or furniture. About all that is needed is to sand any drywall seams and to caulk around any openings. The paint can then be sprayed or rolled on walls and applied by brush around cabinets, windows, and door frames. The time required to paint a new home can be as short as three to six working days or as long as a month. Most often, only one layer of paint is applied per day, so the paint will have time to dry overnight. The required time is based on the size of the project, the preparations required, the number of paint laborers, the amount of specialized work, and sometimes the weather.

The time necessary to repaint or do refurbishing work on an existing home or commercial project could actually take longer than new construction because of repairs and lengthy preparations. Every surface has to be protected and covered when painting in existing rooms. Both spray painting and using a roller will splatter tiny droplets of paint in every direction. That means that all furniture either has to be moved to the center of the room and covered or moved completely out of the room. It also means that all window panes and carpeting have to be completely covered with paper and tarps. After everything is covered, then the patching, caulking, and sanding can begin. Preparations could take several days, but the actual painting could take only several hours. Again the required time for the job will be based on the size of the project, the extent of the preparation, the number of paint laborers, and the amount of specialized work.

Weather can have a major effect on the timing of painting projects. Windy weather can cause insects and dirt to become embedded in wet paint surfaces, requiring extensive touch-up work. In hot and humid weather conditions, painted surfaces take much longer to dry than usual (this is especially true for solvent-based paints). When there are several coats of paint to apply and the weather is humid, the painting process can take several days or weeks. If the temperature is below 50 degrees, you will have to postpone work on exterior or unheated interiors; the cold temperature prevents the paint from correctly adhering to the surfaces.

When estimating time for paint jobs, remember to consider the previous factors carefully.

CHOOSING A PAINTER

After the client has approved the design by giving you a 50 percent deposit and selected paint colors for a project, you will need to hire a painter. It is a good idea to have a few painters in mind before you actually need them so you do not have to waste valuable time collecting references in the middle of a project.

Finding a good painting craftsperson takes a little research, but it is well worth the effort to find a painter you can count on for beautiful, quality work. Start your research by asking for referrals from other interior designers and paint stores. Check the local Yellow Pages under designer sources. After finding two or three promising prospects, set up appointments with them to discuss their various services.

Some painters just do basic painting and are not versed in the complicated painting techniques so many designers want to use. However, decorative painters are available, and most have photographs and samples of previous work they can show you during an interview. When interviewing a decorative painter, ask if he or she can prepare samples for each project for both you and the client to review before the work begins. This ensures that clear communication is taking place. Be sure to ask for client references, especially the names of other designers. Call all references and write down the comments from each reference. Make a file for each person you have decided to use and keep this information current, adding notes from time to time.

On the first few jobs you assign a painter, visit the job site while the painting is in progress. Make notes of the workmanship, neatness of the application, attitude toward you and the client, and the completion of the job to specifications. Always get a signed work order before any work begins to prevent misunderstandings later. As your professional relationship builds, trust on both sides will contribute to a rewarding long-term working relationship.

EXAMPLE OF FINAL PAINTING COSTS

Mrs. Bruno has asked her designer to give her an estimate to paint her master-bedroom walls and baseboards in the spring. The walls are drywall and in good condition, with only nail holes and a few small cracks needing repairs. (This would classify as a standard job with no unusual situations.)

The bedroom is 14 feet by 16 feet with 8-foot ceilings; it has four windows without wood frames, two entry doors, and one bathroom door. The walls are to be painted twice with a custom-colored burgundy flat latex paint; the baseboards will have the same color in semigloss latex paint. The painter and his assistant are very experienced craftspeople.

Room Measurements

Walls: 14' + 16' + 14' + 16' = 60' x 8' ceiling = 480 square feet
Baseboards: 14' + 16' + 14' + 16' = 60 linear feet ·

According to the Paint/Labor Chart on page 20 a room of these measurements would require two gallons of flat latex paint to apply two coats by roller on the walls and one quart of semigloss latex paint to apply two coats by brush on the baseboards.

Final Estimate. After all the measuring, calculating, and estimating has been accomplished, the final figures need to be presented to the client in a contract. The final figures would look something like this:

Labor: Standard job with average preparation, cover walls with two rolled-on coats of dark, custom-colored flat latex paint; cover baseboards with two brushed-on coats of custom-colored semigloss latex paint; touch up and cleanup for 480 suare feet and 60 linear feet.

Estimated Time: 3 hours @ $ 35.00 *	$105.00
Materials: 2 gallons custom-colored flat latex @25.00	50.00
1 quart custom-colored semigloss @15.00	15.00
Other consumable materials	25.00
Overhead: Ten percent	19.50
Profit: Ten percent	21.45
Subtotal	235.95
Tax 7.5% **	17.69
TOTAL	$253.64

* All figures are based on 2001 Phoenix, Arizona prices.
** Each state would calculate tax differently according to their laws. Some states charge tax on newly manufactured products only, not labor. Check your state laws to see what sales and use taxes apply.

Paint Work Order

Date: March 3, 2001
P.O. #: 1065
Designer: Carol Sampson
Address: 244 E. Vista View, Phoenix AZ
Phone: (480) 759-0001

Installation Address: Jennie Bruno
1172 Tulane
Scottsdale, AZ
Phone: (480) 723-6112

Date Promised: March 12, 2001
Painter: Cass Robertson
Address: 4551 Montebello, Phoenix AZ
Phone: (623) 941-8900

No.	Room	Walls North	East	South	West	Ceiling	Trim	Cabinets	Doors	Primer or Base Coat	No. of Paint Coats	Finish Coat	Pre	Semi Gloss	High Gloss	Wall Repairs	Paint Co.	Special Equipment
1	Lvg Rm	✓	✓	✓	✓	Ø	all	Ø	3	Ø	2	Ø	All Trim		Ø	yes	Pro Lux	Ø

Application:
Roller ✓
Brush ✓
Sprayed
Special

Quality of Workmanship:
Premium
Standard ✓
Minimum

Special Instructions: Please cover or remove all furniture, repair nail holes and small cracks around windows — Thanks, Carol

Attach Paint Chip: Sunset Beige

26

Paint Work Order

Date: _____   Installation   Date Promised: _____
P.O. #: _____   Address: _____   Painter: _____
Designer: _____   _____   Address: _____
Address: _____   _____   _____
Phone: _____   Phone: _____   Phone: _____

No.	Room	Walls				Ceiling	Trim	Cabinets	Doors	Primer or Base Coat	No. of Paint Coats	Finish Coat	Flat	Semi Gloss	High Gloss	Wall Repairs	Paint Co.	Special Equipment
		North	East	South	West													

Application:

Roller

Brush

Sprayed

Special

Quality of Workmanship:

Premium:

Standard:

Minimum:

Special Instructions:

Attach Paint Chip:

Chapter Two
WALL COVERINGS

A wallpaper mural in an otherwise blank end wall in a breakfast area pulls you into a peaceful setting.

Wall coverings have been part of interior decoration for over 2,000 years. Beautiful and delicate wallpapers existed in China as early as 200 B.C. These were hand-painted on thin rice paper and then mounted on either linen or silk. Natural scenes with flowers and birds were common themes, as were scenes depicting the legendary exploits of ruling families. Unfortunately, only the rich were able to afford these elegant wall coverings.

Before trade with China was established in the sixteenth century, Europeans had been covering their plastered walls with leather tooled squares, carved wood paneling, and heavy, elaborate tapestries. Once the Chinese wallpapers had been imported, they dominated the wallpaper market in Europe until 1620, when a Frenchman named Le Francois invented the first "poor man's tapestry"—a process that imitated wall-hung velvets and brocades. This process involved printing a pattern in varnish on colored paper, then sprinkling powder-dyed wool shreds onto the wet varnish. When the varnish dried, the excess wool was brushed away This first flocked wallpaper found instant success in France, England, and the United States. From that time until the late eighteenth century the French dominated the wallpaper market.

Late in the seventeenth century, another Frenchman, Jean Papillion, invented a method of block-printing patterns on colored papers. He carved a pattern onto several large wood blocks, then covered each block with paint and pressed it against the paper. The papers were available in any designed color, and the patterns were designed so that they matched up on all sides of each succeeding paper. This method was called straight repeat pattern matching; it increased the adaptability and use of wallpapers all around a room.

In both the United States and Europe, the mid-eighteenth century saw decorative wallpapers designed in a continuous scene or pictorial style. Antique scenics had sets of strips 19 inches wide and 6 to 10 feet long. A specific theme was hung by using connecting panels or strips of paper. Ancient ruins, famous cities, seascapes, landscapes, gardens, villages, and scenes from mythology were all popular themes.

The Industrial Revolution affected the way many products were manufactured, and wallpapers were not excluded. Mass-production of wallpaper began; printing rollers with designs cut into them were inked and rolled onto long paper rolls. This process reduced the manufacturer's costs, but it also lowered the quality by sacrificing the beautiful craftsmanship and attention to detail seen in the antique wallpapers. Only within the last fifty years have high quality wallpapers again become appreciated and requested items for interiors.

WALLPAPER BASICS

Today's wallpapers come in a wide variety of styles, colors, patterns, textures, and prices—from inexpensive manufactured cloth-backed vinyl to costly custom-designed hand-screened papers. Because there is such a broad range of products available, it is important for interior designers to understand some basic information about wallpaper construction and materials to be able to specify appropriate choices.

Printing Techniques. There are two basic wallcovering printing techniques: machine printing and hand-printing. Machine-printed wallpapers are the less expensive of the two due to the ease and speed of the manufacturing process. Hand-printed wallpapers require manual labor for each color applied to the design and therefore cost much more to manufacture. Both machine-printed and hand-printed wallcoverings can be custom-made.

Machine-Made wallcoverings. There are four major types of machine-printing processes: rotogravure, surface, flexographic, and rotary screen.

Rotogravure creates a technically consistent, flat, machined look and feel to the wallpaper surface. The design is engraved onto the surface of metal cylinders-one cylinder for each color. Fast-drying paint colors are trapped in the engraved indentation and rolled onto a paper or vinyl wallcovering material. Heat is then applied to the moving strip of wallcovering material to speed up the drying of each color before the next cylinder applies the succeeding color of the design. Generally this printing process uses no more than six colors, which keeps this type of wallcovering inexpensive.

Surface printing involves the use of metal cylinders with a raised design. Surface printing gives a textured, hand-painted look to a machine-made wallcovering, but with a cost-effective machine process. It creates the eye appeal of the randomness of original art. Surface printed can have up to twelve colors, with one cylinder per color. Again, fast-drying paints are used and heat is applied to the moving strip of wallcovering material, either a vinyl or paper.

Flexographic printing is a type of surface printing using a limited number of colors (most often one to four colors are used). Raised designs are engraved onto a plastic composition cylinder, while the base is cut away Colored ink adheres to the raised areas and is rolled onto a paper or vinyl wallcovering material. The printed design has the clean appearance of a block print.

Rotary-screen printing uses a mesh formed into a cylinder, onto which the design is applied. Ink is pushed from the inside of the cylinder through to the wallcovering surface material. This style of printing gives a hand-printed look with a clean, crisp, finished appearance. However, register marks must be carefully set to ensure that each color aligns in the correct pattern placement during this high-speed printing process.

Hand-Printed wallcoverings. There are two types of hand-printed wallcovers: hand-block and silk-screened.

The hand-block printing process uses a separate wood block for each motif in a

Contemporary wallpaper.

repeat. A raised pattern is created on the block; ink is applied to the surface of the pattern, and the block is then pressed onto the paper. This was the first wallcovering printing process used. It is rarely used now because it is very time-consuming and expensive.

Silk-screened wallcoverings are elaborate, beautiful, and expensive. Each pattern color has its own wooden silk-screen frame made for the width of the wallcovering material, usually 30 inches. Each wooden frame has a piece of silk tightly stretched across it with a pattern drawn for each color and the remaining silk blocked out with a varnish. These silk-screen frames are separately laid onto a long piece of paper strip, and colored ink is then pushed through the screen onto the paper. Each color of the pattern is applied one by one down the strip of paper, with drying time allowed between each application. Highlights or additional shadings of the design can be produced by overprinting any part the design. Small irregularities are expected; they give assurance that the paper is handmade. The most expensive silk-screened papers can have fifteen to thirty colors, creating virtual works of art. Silk-screened wallcoverings usually need to be trimmed at each side, which adds extra labor costs to the final cost of installation.

Custom wallcoverings. Custom-made means one-of-a-kind, never before done. When custom-colored papers are specified, the manufacturer will always require a minimum order. There will also be an up-front charge to manufacture a custom-made paper. Additionally there will be a charge for a strike-off, which entails setting up the dyes and printing one strip for customer approval before the rest of the rollage is actually printed. Sometimes, when the design is perfect, but the colors need changing, there is no other solution except to specify custom wallpapering.

Wallcovering Materials. Today's wallpapers are made from a variety of materials, each for different purposes. Many of the materials can be machine-printed or silk-screened and most can be washed or gently vacuumed.

Vinyl wallcoverings come in a broad price range and can be machine-printed or silk-screened. They are the most durable wallcoverings; they will stand up to repeated scrubbing and cleaning. This durability makes them most desirable for kitchens and bathrooms. There are three types of vinyl wallcoverings. The first is a vinyl sheet laminated to a paper back (this is easiest to strip when changing wallpaper). The second is a vinyl sheet laminated to a cloth back (this is the easiest to hang). The third is a vinyl-impregnated cloth with a paper back (expanded vinyl papers have a heavy textured raised surface on the face of the wallcovering as opposed to a smoother printed design with ink). Many commercial-grade, vinyl wallcoverings have protective coatings that help the product stay clean and ensure long-lasting wear. Du Pont manufactures a brand-name product called Tedlar—a .0005-inch-thick, clear, polyvinyl fluoride film. When this film is laminated to certain vinyl wallcoverings, it protects the colors and patterns nearly as well as cleaning glass or ceramic tile. Coated wallcoverings protected with Tedlar are ideal for hospitality and healthcare facilities—especially in corridors and cafeterias where the walls take a lot of abuse. Durability ratings for vinyl wallcoverings are calculated according to their weight rather than type; they range from a rating of modest durability, 12 to 15 ounce, up to a rating of very durable, 21 to 26 ounce, for heavily-used corridors.

When hanging vinyl wallpaper, vinyl paste is applied sparingly because vinyls are nonbreathing: they will mildew if wheat paste or excessive paste is used. Also take care not to stretch the paper when hanging, otherwise, when the paste dries, the paper will shrink and the seams will pop open.

Paper wallcoverings can be either machine-printed or silk-screened. They tend to be more delicate than vinyl and are not able to take a lot of scrubbing. These papers are best used in low-maintenance areas such as living rooms, dining rooms, and bedrooms.

Flocked wallcoverings can be either machine-printed or silk-screened. Today's flock fibers are made from rayon and nylon and are washable. When flocked wallcoverings are hung or cleaned, do not brush against them; excessive rubbing will flatten the flock.

Foil wallcoverings come in two types, aluminum laminated to paper and simulated metallic, and these can be either machine-printed or silk-screened. Foil can be washed with a mild cleaner and must be dried with a soft towel. Because foils will show every imperfection—from nail holes to tiny scratches—they need to be

Striped wallpaper hung horizontally.

hung on perfectly smooth walls. Before foils are hung, the walls should be sponged with a household bleach to kill any bacteria that could cause tarnishing or corrosion on the metallic inks. Like vinyl wallcoverings, foils are nonbreathing and require a vinyl paste for installation. If a wheat paste is used there is a possibility of mildewing and staining.

Grasscloth is an oriental import made from long, natural grass harvested for this purpose. The grasses are knotted together and then handwoven on homemade looms. The grasses are either dyed in small batches or left natural, and then glued to a natural or colored backing of rice paper. A roll of grasscloth will always have a variation of color throughout: this is the natural inherent quality of this type of handmade paper. An uneven look can be avoided by hanging strips of grasscloth in an alternating manner, with each successive strip turned opposite in rotation for a blended effect. Grasscloth can be gently vacuumed for cleaning.

Hemp, tulu, and burlap are oriental imports as well. They are handmade from different types of grasses and are loom woven. These grasses can also be dyed or left natural and glued with a water-soluble glue to natural or colored papers. All of these oriental imported papers are delicate and unwashable, and will fade if exposed to sunlight. When hanging these grasses, take care not to saturate the paper with too much paste or the paper backing will separate from the woven grasscloth.

String wallcoverings are a fairly new treatment within the history of wallpapers. Strings in various colors, sizes, and textures are glued to a colored paper backing that moves along an assembly line. The strings are kept immobile while heat dries the glue. Seams rarely show with string wallcoverings.

Borders are narrow wallpaper strips from 2 to 12 inches wide. They are hung on walls at the ceiling level, at chair-rail height, at baseboards, and around windows. Borders are packaged in 5-yard spools.

A mural wallcovering is a single subject usually printed across several strips of paper. There are three common types of murals: photo murals, scenics, and antique documentaries. The photo murals are photographs of any subject matter scaled large enough to fill an entire wall. Scenics come in all styles and price ranges, from inexpensive vinyl scenics to expensive paper scenes of gardens, cities, or landscapes. The antique or documentary murals were generally made from linens and rag papers with designs of the eighteenth century.

Blank paper stock—also called wall lining—is used to smooth out damaged walls and to protect decorative papers from absorbing any discoloration from plaster walls. Blank stock is often used under antique or expensive scenic wallpapers to permit removal of the wallpaper without tearing it.

Commercial wallpapers are 54 inches wide and are generally in vinyl textures and designed with a minimal use of patterns.

Wallpaper Books. Wallpaper books are sample books used by wallpaper manufacturers to sell their different wallpapers. These are very useful to the designer as they enable the client to see the many options available for a particular type of wallpaper. In addition to the wallpaper samples, every wallpaper book has specific information regarding the installation and care requirements pertaining to the wallpapers within that book. For instance, a designer specifying a paper for a kitchen or bathroom will need to know whether the surface is scrubbable. Scrubbable papers have a stain-resistant coating of a plastic or vinyl applied to their surface for maintenance-free use. wallcoverings that are strippable require no steaming or scraping to remove. Pretrimmed wallcoverings have had their edges trimmed before packaging and are ready for installation. Silk-screened papers always need trimming to cut away edges where the register marks were used in the printing process. Prepasted papers have had the adhesive pretreated before packaging; however most professional wallpaper hangers will paste prepasted papers for a truly tight installation.

Most wallpapers today have a fire rating printed in their book. Nearly all papers can be used for both residential and commercial projects; however any wallpaper used in a commercial project must be rated for flammability.

Fabrics as wallcoverings. There are several ways to hang fabrics as wallcoverings. Certain companies will apply a special backing to any fabric to make it suitable for hanging on a wall, or paper can be laminated to the back of a fabric and then hung on the wall (all fabrics used in this way need to be preshrunk). When hanging fabrics, take care not to stretch the back of the fabric or to use excessive glue that could seep through to the face of the fabric or through the butted seams.

Vinylizing the face of a fabric will create a "wet look" suitable for bathrooms or kitchens. Fabrics can also be foam-backed to give the finished walls an upholstered look. Foam-backed fabrics can help to even out wall surfaces and are good for acoustical sound dampening.

WALL PREPARATIONS

All walls must be properly prepared before new wallcoverings can be hung. Whether new or old, the walls must be clean and dry, meaning free from grease, dirt, body oils, and old wallpaper. Wall preparation can be done by the client or the paper hanger depending on the budget for the job (this choice needs to be made by the client because wall preparations will add extra labor costs to the installation). Nail holes and cracks in walls need to be repaired with patching plaster or spackling compound. Then, these patched areas must be sized and spot-painted so the surface is a uniform color and texture. Walls should be smooth, as any irregularities in their surface will show up in subsequent wallpapering (foil papers especially show every imperfection as the light hits the shining wallpaper surface).

Old wallpaper must be removed before new can be applied. If old wallpapers are left on the surface, their inks may bleed through the new papers, and any bright pattern or textured paper using metallic inks will tarnish and show through. Finally new wallpaper will not adhere to the surface of an older vinyl wallcovering; the new paper will literally fall off.

Porous or unsealed surfaces of both plaster and drywall must be sized, primed, or sealed. This will provide better adhesion when wallpaper is applied. New plaster walls must cure for thirty to sixty days and then be neutralized with zinc sulfate or sized with an oil-based wall sealer. All drywall joints must be taped and any holes smoothed with patching plaster, then sanded, and a coat of sizing applied. A common primer for drywall is a latex acrylic.

There are many prepared wall sizing or glue sizing products available on the market today. Check with a wallpaper dealer or hanger for the best one for each job. Before applying wallpaper to a painted surface, the surface must be sanded so that the wallpaper will adhere to it. Enameled or glossy surfaces must be washed first with a household antiseptic and then dulled by sanding. If the walls are dark in color, they will need to be painted with a light color or hung with blank stock to keep the dark color from showing through the new wallcovering. Finally the trim and other adjacent areas that are not being papered should be painted before the wallcoverings are hung.

ESTIMATING MATERIALS

Understanding basic wallcovering estimating and costs allows the designer to make sure that enough material has been ordered to complete the job. The ability to estimate will also allow the client to make choices during the design process, knowing how his or her choices will affect the budget rather than finding out when it is too late to make changes.

How To Measure for Wallpapers. Accurate measurements are of primary importance in figuring wallpaper rollage. Always use a steel tape measure, preferably 16 to 25 feet long with a 3/4-inch-wide blade. This type of measuring tape will remain stiff as it is pushed up a wall or along the floor. *Always measure in inches.*

While measuring for wallcoverings can be done in several ways, the safest way is to measure the length and then the width of each wall. Put these room measurements on a rough sketch or graph paper. The clearest room plan shows the floor in the center and the walls extending from it laid flat. Measure windows, doors, and fireplace openings, then record these measurements on the drawing. A copy of this diagram should be kept in the client's file for reference. (A follow-up remeasure should also be made by the wallpaper hanger to guarantee final accuracy and to spell out any technical details needed before the wallpaper is ordered.)

Estimating Wallpaper. Estimating wallpaper can be done using one of three methods: consulting manufacturer's charts, using the strip method, or using the square-footage method. The fastest and easiest method is to consult a chart. Convenient charts can be found in some wallpaper books. Most charts are based on 30 square feet of coverage per single roll of wallcovering. Manufacturers ship 36 square feet of material per single roll. The 6-square-foot deduction provides for normal cutting and ceiling level matching during trimming and hanging. For average rooms in a basic box shape, this method works fine.

The second method is to estimate by the strip method. This is used mainly by professional wallpaper hangers in rooms with chopped up wall spaces or cathedral ceilings, and in large commercial installations. The strip method requires literally counting the actual strips to be used in any situation. It is much more difficult for the novice to use and not recommended as a common practice. Many elements enter into the total rollage such as using some waste strips in shorter wall areas.

The final method is to determine the square footage. The square-footage process will work for almost any wall surface to be covered by wallcoverings. (This method will be used in this chapter to demonstrate wallpaper estimating.)

The amount of wallpaper or coverage needed for each room or individual wall is determined by the width of the wallpaper and any pattern repeat. There are four types of wallpaper available with different widths: European, 20 to 22 inches wide; American-made, 27 inches wide; Oriental wovens (grasscloth, etc.), 36 inches wide; and Commercial, 54 inches wide.

Most wallpapers are packaged with two or three rolls to the bolt in a continuous roll. Multiple-roll bolts reduce the amount of waste when hanging versus a single roll. One roll of wallpaper only has two and a half strips when there is an 8-foot

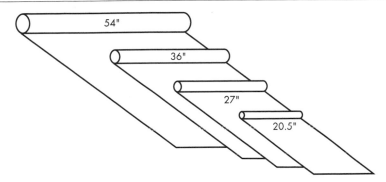

ceiling. The double-roll wallpaper has five full strips based on an 8-foot ceiling.

Quite often it is necessary to order an odd number of rolls. When this occurs, the manufacturer will charge an extra two or three dollars to open a double bolt, cut it in half, and rewrap it.

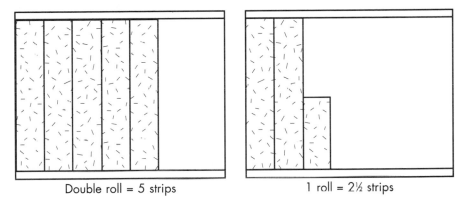

Double roll = 5 strips   1 roll = 2½ strips

It is best to have extra rollage for every wallpaper job. The possibility always exists that some of the measurements are inaccurate or that a strip or two might become damaged during the cutting process. In addition, two extra rolls should always be ordered to ensure that the client will have matching paper for any later repairs. Subsequent dye lots are not guaranteed to match original orders, and the color often vanes.

Before the wallpaper is cut, be certain there is sufficient yardage to complete the desired installation and that there are no flaws in the paper. No manufacturer will accept cut bolts or single bolts for a refund. Extra wallpaper must be sent back within thirty days of the purchase. A restocking fee will be charged.

American-Made wallcoverings. There is a standard formula for estimating American-made (27-inch-wide) wallpaper for one wall of a square room. Note: This basic formula will only work for American-made wallpapers without a pattern repeat. Measure the perimeter or distance around the room, multiply that measurement by the height of the ceiling, and then divide by 30. It is a standard practice to deduct two single rolls of wallpaper for every four ordinary openings in the room: windows, doors, and closets.

Example: The room is 12 feet by 14 feet with 8-foot ceilings and the wallpaper is a plain American-made 27-inch-wide paper with no pattern repeat. The room has two windows and two doors.

12' + 14' + 12' + 14' = 52' x 8' ceiling = 416' ÷ 30 = 14 rolls

Deduct 2 rolls for 4 openings leaving 12 rolls.

In a standard, box-shaped room this formula works perfectly. However, in an unusual room with angles, curves, cathedral ceilings, or other architectural features, precautions need to be taken. The above process can leave the installation short of wallpaper when unusual wall sizes are encountered. In these situations you can sometimes mix methods. For a standard box-shaped room with an unusual alcove, use the square-foot method for the box-shaped three sides of the room and the strip method for the alcove side and then add them together. In situations where the whole space is unusual and complex, common sense should prevail and a professional paper hanger consulted to estimate the paper before ordering.

European wallcoverings. European (20–22-inch-wide) rollage is estimated by figuring square footage and then dividing by 22. When using European papers, more rollage is needed than when using American-made 27-inch-wide wallpapers.

Example: The room is 12 feet by 14 feet with 8-foot ceilings. The room has two windows and two doors.

12' + 14' + 12' + 14' = 52' x 8' ceiling 416' ÷ 22 = 18 rolls

Deduct 2 rolls for 4 openings leaving a total of 16 rolls.

Oriental wallcoverings. Estimating for imported oriental (36-inch-wide) wallpaper is done using the square-footage method and then dividing by 36. Oriental wallpapers are always handwoven using 36-inch-wide papers and do not have much waste.

Example: The room is 12 feet by 14 feet with 8-foot ceilings. The room has two windows and two doors.

12' + 14' + 12' + 14' = 52' x 8' ceiling = 416' ÷ 36 = 12 rolls

Deduct 2 rolls for 4 openings leaving a total of 10 rolls.

Commercial wallcoverings. Estimating for commercial (54-inch-wide) wallcovering can be done by the strip method or by the square-footage method and then dividing the result by 13.5 to convert the measurement to linear yards. The square-footage estimate has to be converted to linear yards for ordering since this is the only way commercial papers are manufactured and sold.

Example: The office is 25 feet by 40 feet with 8-foot ceilings. The office has no windows and two doors.

5' + 40' + 25' + 40' = 130' x 8' ceiling = 1,404' ÷ 13.5 = 77 linear yards

Deductions for openings are usually not made for commercial wallcoverings. The 54" wallcovering would be wider than most door openings or windows

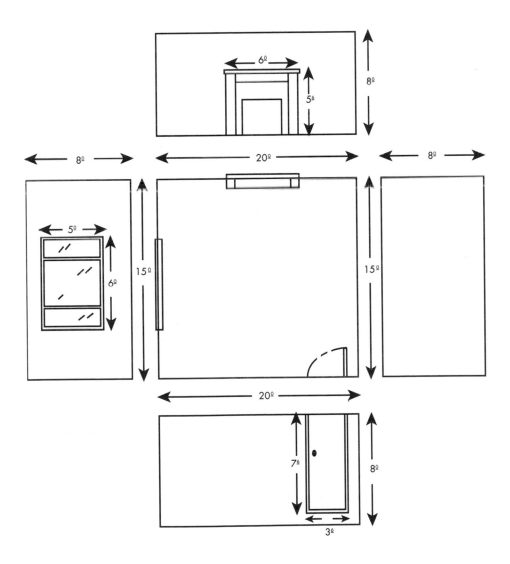

Pattern Repeats. Most wallpapers will have a pattern repeat. A pattern repeat is the lengthwise or crosswise measurement of one design motif to where that same pattern is again repeated. There are three types of pattern repeats: straight, half-drop, and random.

Straight. The straight pattern repeat has a straight-across match and can have a repeat from 1 to 36 inches. The larger the repeat, the more wallpaper is needed to match up the pattern.

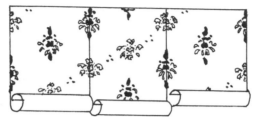

Half drop. The half-drop pattern repeat has the same height pattern motif halfway in between two other repeats. On the half-drop repeat, the pattern appears to have diagonal lines.

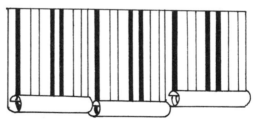

Random. The plain or random pattern match does not present a matching problem for wallpapering. However, it is advisable to reverse strips when hanging grass-cloth wallpapers.

Estimating pattern repeats for American papers is a simple procedure. Measure the distance between the repeats. If the repeat is every 18 inches or less, the total square footage is divided by 30. If the pattern repeat is over 18 inches, the total square footage is divided by 25.

Example: The room is 12' + 14 + 12' + 14' = 52' x 8' ceiling = 416' ÷ 25 = 16 rolls

Deduct 2 rolls for 4 openings for a total of 14 rolls.

Rollage Chart. The following chart will enable you to estimate wallpaper rollage for plain or solid papers. However, any papers that are pattern repeated will still require a formula.

ROLLAGE CHART

Size of Room	Single Rolls 8-Foot Ceiling (2.4m)							Single Rolls 9-Foot Ceiling (2.7m)						
	Euro	Am	Oriental	Commercial (yards)	Metric	Ceiling	Border (yards)	Euro	Am	Oriental	Comm. (yards)	Metric	Ceiling	Border (yards)
8 × 10	13	10	8	21 yards	9	4	13	15	10	9	24 yards	10	4	13
10 × 12	16	12	10	26 yards	11	4	16	18	13	11	29 yards	12	4	16
12 × 12	17	13	11	28 yards	12	5	17	20	14	12	32 yards	14	5	17
12 × 14	19	14	12	31 yards	13	6	18	21	16	13	35 yards	15	6	18
12 × 16	20	15	12	33 yards	14	6	20	23	17	14	37 yards	16	6	20
14 × 16	22	16	13	35 yards	15	7	22	25	18	15	40 yards	17	7	22
14 × 18	23	17	14	38 yards	16	8	23	26	19	16	43 yards	18	8	23
14 × 20	24	18	15	40 yards	17	9	25	28	20	17	45 yards	19	9	25
16 × 22	28	20	17	45 yards	19	11	27	31	22	19	50 yards	21	11	27
16 × 24	29	21	18	47 yards	20	12	29	33	24	20	53 yards	22	12	29
18 × 24	31	22	19	50 yards	21	14	31	34	25	21	56 yards	23	14	31
20 × 24	32	23	20	52 yards	22	16	32	36	26	22	59 yards	25	16	32
20 × 30	36	27	22	59 yards	25	20	36	41	30	25	67 yards	28	20	36

ROLLAGE CHART

Size of Room	Single Rolls – 10-Foot Ceiling (2.4m)							Single Rolls – 12-Foot Ceiling (2.7m)						
	Euro	Am	Oriental	Commercial (yards)	Metric	Ceiling	Border (yards)	Euro	Am	Oriental	Comm. (yards)	Metric	Ceiling	Border (yards)
8 × 10	16	12	10	27 yards	11	4	13	20	14	12	32 yards	13	4	13
10 × 12	20	15	12	33 yards	14	4	16	24	18	15	39 yards	16	4	16
12 × 12	22	16	13	36 yards	15	5	17	26	19	16	43 yards	18	5	17
12 × 14	24	17	14	39 yards	16	6	18	28	21	17	46 yards	19	6	18
12 × 16	25	19	16	41 yards	17	6	20	31	22	19	50 yards	21	6	20
14 × 16	27	20	17	44 yards	19	7	22	33	24	20	53 yards	22	7	22
14 × 18	29	21	18	47 yards	20	8	23	35	26	21	57 yards	24	8	23
14 × 20	31	23	19	50 yards	21	9	25	37	27	23	60 yards	25	9	25
16 × 22	35	25	21	56 yards	23	11	27	41	30	25	68 yards	28	11	27
16 × 24	36	27	22	59 yards	25	12	29	44	32	27	71 yards	30	12	29
18 × 24	38	28	23	62 yards	26	14	31	46	34	28	75 yards	31	14	31
20 × 24	40	29	24	65 yards	27	16	32	48	35	29	78 yards	32	16	32
20 × 30	45	33	28	74 yards	28	20	36	55	40	33	89 yards	33	20	36

TIME ESTIMATING

The installation of wall covering is always an exciting time for a client because it changes any room's personality Most clients are both excited and anxious to see how the room will look. However, a realistic time estimate to complete the installation can only be given after the wallcovering has been ordered. Often, the client's chosen wallpaper will be back-ordered, which will delay the installation. After the contract is signed and the client has given you a 50 percent deposit, order the wallpaper. If the stock is available, it will take about five to ten working days to receive the order. During that time, you should call the paper hanger in to set up an installation date.

The actual time it will take to hang the paper depends on how many helpers the paper hanger has on his or her team. If there is no furniture to move, the job will go faster. Most single paper hangers can hang between 15 to 25 rolls a day. They are slowed up if they have to trim paper or cut around cabinets (as in kitchens and bathrooms). Ask the paper hanger for an estimated time for installation and let the client know that time.

COST ESTIMATING

Estimating costs for wallcoverings involves two main factors: the materials and hanging labor. Wallpaper can vary widely in price, ranging from 12 to 200 dollars per roll, depending on the type and style of paper. Labor is charged per roll rather than per hour, and can cost anywhere from 20 to 40 dollars a roll to hang, depending on the type of paper and the difficulty of the job; prices are also subject to the local economy.

CHOOSING A PAPER HANGER

After the wallpaper is decided upon by the client, unless he or she intends to do the work, the designer must hire a subcontractor to hang the paper. A good designer usually has a number of different subcontractors he or she likes to work with. It is advisable to have people in mind before you need them so you are not first getting referrals when a job needs to be completed next week.

The choice of a paper hanger is varied and wide, ranging from inexpensive part-timers to seasoned professionals. Discernment is the key in selecting a good paper hanger. Begin by getting referrals from other professional interior designers. (Some designers will share their sources and others are not as generous.) Another way to find paper hangers is through a paint and paper store. The stores will give out several paper hangers' cards with recommendations about their qualifications. Well-qualified paper hangers can hang all types of wallpaper, including the difficult decorator papers that need extra trimming and matching.

After finding two or three prospective paper hangers, set up appointments for interviews. During these interviews, find out what types of papers the paper hangers enjoy hanging and the kinds they do not want to hang. This information will reveal his or her attitude towards the job and if he or she will hang decorator papers that need more time and attention. Request their list of referrals, labor charges, and extras such as: papering outlets and switch plate covers, papering registers, trip charges, removing and re-hanging large mirrors and/or lighting fixtures and moving any furniture. Also, ask if they work with both residential and commercial projects, and if they give discounts for large jobs.

Good paper hangers will be happy to provide a list of satisfied clients. Call every referral and get specific information for your files. It is wise to have the names of two or three qualified paper hangers so that if one is unavailable, you have others to call.

When you find a paper hanger and hire him or her for a job, always get a signed work order to avoid misunderstandings, and always visit the job site to check on the progress and the workmanship. Look to make sure that the patterns are straight and matching, the seams do not separate, and the cleanup is to everyone's satisfaction. Keep a file for each person you decide to give work to and keep comments on his or her performance. This record will help you make a decision the next time you need to hire a paper hanger.

EXAMPLE OF FINAL WALLCOVERING COSTS

Mr. and Mrs. McDonald have hired a designer to help them coordinate the installation of a wallpaper in their living room. There is an existing wallpaper that must be stripped, plus nail holes and cracks that need to be repaired on all of the walls. The walls need to be extremely smooth because the new wallpaper the McDonalds have selected will show any flaws in the wall surface. Since the walls are going to be resurfaced, they will also need sizing.

The wallpaper chosen for the living room is an American brand with a pattern repeat of 24 inches. Their living room measures 16 feet by 23 feet and has 10-foot ceilings, two large windows, and two large doorways.

Use formulas for this estimate; the chart will not calculate pattern repeats.

Room Measurements

Walls: 16' + 23' + 16' + 23' = 78' x 10' ceilings = 780 square feet

Repeat is 24 inches apart so divide by 25. 780 ÷ 25 = 32 rolls. Deduct 2 rolls for 4 openings leaving a total of 30 rolls.

Final Estimate. After all the measuring, calculating, and estimating have been accomplished, the final figures for the living room would look something like this:

Labor: Strip old wallpaper and repair nail holes and cracks, etc.; will vary depending on the subcontractor	$300.00*
Size all walls per roll; 30 single rolls @ $5.00	150.00
Hang wallpaper; 30 single rolls @ $25.00	750.00
Wallpaper: Pattern – 5665 Seville; color – Champagne; 30 single rolls @ $36.00	1,080.00
Subtotal	$2,280.00
Tax 7.5% **	171.00
TOTAL	$2,451.00

Estimated time to remove old wallpaper and install new paper, 2 to 5 days after wallpaper has been received.

* All figures are based on 2001 Phoenix, Arizona prices.

** Each state would calculate tax differently according to their laws. Some states apply tax to newly manufactured products only, not to labor. Check your state laws to see what sales and use taxes apply.

Wallpaper Work Order

Date: March 3, 2001
P.O. # 1075
Designer: Carol Sampson
Address: 244 E. Vista View
Phoenix, AZ 85048
(480) 759-0001
Phone:

Address:

Phone:

Wallpaper Installer: Gary Hollbrook
Date Promised: March 14, 2001
Address: Vista View
Phoenix, AZ
(623) 932-2000
Phone:

Customer: Betty Wager
734 Seville Lane
Scottsdale, AZ
(480) 975-7713

Room	Walls				Pattern No.	Repeat	Type of Paper	Rollage or Yards	Trimmed Paper	Remove Paper	No. of Switch Plates	Blank Stock/ Sizing	Labor Price/ Roll
	North	East	South	West									
1. Living	✓	✓	✓	✓	Seville	24"	Deco Paper	30 S/R	No	yes	6	Sizing	25.00
2.													
3.													
4.													
5.													
6.													
7.													
8.													
9.													
10.													

P.S. Gary,
Please smooth & repair all walls, fill cracks + nail holes. Paper will be delivered to you, thanks.

Wallpaper Work Order

Date: _____

P.O. #: _____

Designer: _____

Address: _____

Phone: _____

Address: _____

Phone: _____

Wallpaper Installer: _____

Date Promised: _____

Address: _____

Phone: _____

Room	Walls				Pattern No.	Repeat	Type of Paper	Rollage or Yards	Trimmed Paper	Remove Paper	No. of Switch Plates	Sizing Widths	Price Per Roll
	North	East	South	West									
1.													
2.													
3.													
4.													
5.													
6.													
7.													
8.													
9.													
10.													

Chapter Three
CARPETING

Carpet and
slate flooring.

Woven rugs have been in existence for approximately 5,000 years. The ancient Egyptians originated rug weaving for the use of their royalty—pictorial records of ancient Egypt depict patterned rugs in the place of honor before the Pharaoh's throne. In China for the past 4,000 years, the imperial court has treasured their finely woven silk rugs and used them in ceremonial rites. At one time the rugs were used as currency for foreign trade and as diplomatic gifts to the rulers of neighboring countries. Ancient writers such as Homer, Horace, Pliny, and others described the magnificence of Eastern rugs. Further records of rug weaving are found in the Assyrian and Babylonian bas-reliefs of 700 B.C.

Woven rugs reached their peak in popularity and design in Persia between the sixth and thirteenth centuries. The fine, long wool of their rugged highland sheep was perfect for rug weaving. Rugs were woven with colored threads of silk, cotton, linen, or wool knotted to the warp yarns with as many as 1,000 knots per square inch. These rugs, depending on the size, could take longer than a year to weave. Certain towns and cities became famous for particular patterns and designs, which depicted medallions, hunting scenes, and garden patterns, sometimes inlaid with precious stones. The huge royal woven rug of the Persian King Chosroes I(630 A.D.) was made of wool intertwined with gold and silver threads and measured 150 by 75 feet. Intricately designed wool rugs were used for tent walls, partitions, awnings, and hangings. Smaller, simpler, patterned rugs were used as camel saddles, bed mats, covers, and portieres.

Persian medallion or "star" Ushak carpet, Turkey, 1585.

Rug weaving was introduced to Southern Europe during the Moslem invasions into Spain and France in the thirteenth century. The first European rug looms were established in Aubusson, France.

The English were slower to convert to woven rugs, possibly because of their distance from the sources of supply. Plaited rushes and straw covered the floors of English castles and royal palaces during the Middle Ages. Edward III has been credited with introducing rug weaving to England; in about 1350 he brought an entire guild of Flemish Weavers to London. However, the art of rug weaving was not firmly established in England until Queen Elizabeth imported Persian rug makers during her later reign. English patterns adapted the Turkish designs. Two hundred years later, rug weaving guilds were established in England. These guilds set high standards for the craft, and heated competition developed between the guilds at Axminster, Kidderminster, and Wilton in the 1740s.

Persian weavers were also employed by the French court of Henry IV, who, in 1608, set up looms in the Louvre. The famous Savonnerie factory was founded in the early seventeenth century.

French Savannerie carpet, 17th century.

At the same time France was setting up looms in the Louvre, early American settlers were making their own hooked rugs—a patterned rug made by "hooking" yarn or strips of narrow cloth through the back of coarse hemp, linen, or cotton mesh in a technique similar to point embroidery. Made from rags and scraps of old clothes, these colorful rugs were used by average families while the more affluent settlers imported fine woven rugs from England and France.

In 1839, the era of exclusively handwoven rugs ended with the Industrial Revolution, which introduced incredible machinery used to mass-produce carpeting and area rugs. The mechanized speed of the first power loom changed the rug industry overnight in both the United States and Europe. This loom, based on Arkwright's, Cartwright's, and Jacquard's machine designs, used metal hole-punched cards to place the proper color in the design. Wall-to-wall carpet was now available to cover any size room at a price most people could afford.

CARPET BASICS

Today's carpets are made from a number of different fibers—both natural and synthetic—and are available in many different constructions and weaves. Color and pattern possibilities are almost unlimited, within a wide range of quality and price. An understanding of some of the basics about carpet materials will help you when you are estimating and ordering.

Carpet Construction. Several different types of carpet manufacturing have developed since the Industrial Revolution. The three most practical methods are tufting, fusion bonding, and woven process.

Tufting. Although tufted carpeting has only been around since World War II, it now accounts for approximately 80 percent of all carpet manufactured. Tufting is the fastest and most economical method of manufacturing carpet, and as a result, tufted carpet is generally less expensive than woven carpet. The tufting process uses huge sewing machines that insert big stitches, or loops, of pile fiber into a primary backing; this backing is then sealed with a secondary backing, usually latex. Manufacturers often use over a thousand needles in this process. The distance the yarn penetrates beyond the face of the backing determines the pile height.

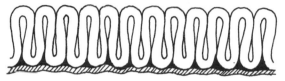

Fusion Bonding. The fusion-bonding method of construction is primarily used for carpet tiles. With fusion bonding, the pile yarn is inserted directly into a liquid vinyl, which then hardens and locks the yarn in place. This construction ensures outstanding tuft lock as well as a continuous, impermeable back. Solid-color and print-base carpeting can be produced using the fusion bonding method. Carpet tiles cost 25 to 40 percent more than broadloom carpet, but will generally wear longer and maintain a better appearance because they can be rotated. In open-plan commercial office areas, where cabling for computers and phones are routed underneath access or raised flooring, carpet tiles are a popular choice because they can be removed easily when the cabling needs to be changed.

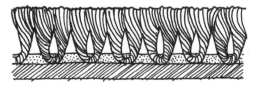

Weaving. The woven process is the most expensive, but it also provides carpets with better wear, better pattern definition, and more dimensional stability than those created by tufting or fusion bonding. In this process, face and backing yarns are woven together simultaneously. There are three methods of weaving: Axminster, Wilton, and velvet.

Axminster. The Axminster method originated in England and employs a mechanical pattern device that selects different colored yarns in sequence from separate spools. This process offers an endless and diverse range of patterns and colors. When planning the installation, it is important to note that the heavy ribbed backing of this carpet only allows it to be rolled lengthwise.

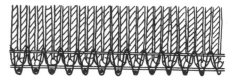

Wilton. The Wilton method also originated in England. This weaving process uses perforated punch cards to control the intricate patterns and feed yarns onto the pile surface. In this process, yarns are woven one at a time and cover up the previous yarns woven so that the finished carpet is given density and durability

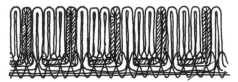

Velvet. The velvet method is the simplest weaving process. Wires are inserted between the pile and warp yarn, and pile height is set according to the height of the inserted wires. This weave also has a thicker backing that makes it more durable. Most velvet carpets are solid colored, although stripes and patterns may be produced by modifying the loom.

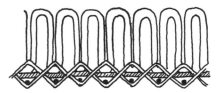

A carpet's density and performance can also be determined by the construction of the yarn. Ply refers to the combining and twisting of two, three, or four yarns. A three-ply yarn generally gives the carpet a thicker and more plush texture than a single-twisted yarn. The tightness of the twist is also a factor in bulk and performance. In general, the more turns per inch, the tighter the twist. Tighter twist gives the carpet less bulk, but better performance. The twist is kept in place by a process called heat setting. Two to four yarns are tightly twisted together while being sub-

jected to extreme heat to hold the twist. When examining carpet, be sure that the tips of individual yarns are neat, tight, and well defined, not loose and flared open.

Pile Fibers

Wool. Wool was the original carpet material, and it is still used as a yardstick that all other fibers are measured against. Wool is more expensive than the manmade fibers of nylon, acrylic, polyester, and olefin that have more recently come into use. However, it has many desirable characteristics including good resiliency, softness, high dyeability, and beauty. Because of its high moisture content, wool is inherently fire resistant. In addition, depending on the construction of the pile, wool carpet can be as durable as nylon.

Nylon. So far, the most successful of all manmade fibers is nylon. Invented in 1938 by DuPont, nylon was first used to make military parachutes because of its extreme strength. Nylon was introduced to the public after World War II, and it has been continually improved upon by many carpet mills. Nylon carpet now represents 80 percent of all carpet sold today. The material's popularity comes from its versatility, its great strength, and its resistance to abrasion; nylon will outlast most if not all natural and manmade fibers in wearability and can be dyed in a wide range of colors. In addition, it is mothproof and resists mildew and mold, making it hypoallergenic.

Fluorochemical stain protectors are available for nylon carpets. These fluorochemical based treatments offer broad-spectrum protection against most water- and oil-based stains by coating the carpet fibers with an "invisible shield" against soil and many common household stains.

The only detrimental feature of nylon is that it generates static electric buildup, which can interfere with the operation of electrical and computer equipment. This problem is controlled by one of three methods: (1) by combining nylon and wool with conductive fibers and a conductive back to discharge static electricity; (2) introducing tiny metallic wire fibers into the yarn before tufting or weaving (this method can also add a decorative appearance to the carpeting); and (3) adding a static-reducing chemical substance to the dye solution (this method is less effective than the others because the chemical will eventually wear off).

Static buildup must be reduced or eliminated in electronic and computer areas, especially in hospitals and nursing homes where medical equipment must function correctly. In areas with medical, electronic, or computer equipment, static generation must be held well below the standard acceptance level of 3.5 kilovolts. *Acrylic.* Acrylic was introduced in 1957 and is often compared to wool. Acrylic fibers possess warmth, durability, softness, fair abrasion resistance, and good crush resistance. Solution-dyed acrylics take bright, clear colors and are especially resistant to sun deterioration. Like all manmade fibers, acrylic is mothproof, resists mildew and mold, and is hypoallergenic. Acrylic is used more in blends than in single-fiber carpets on today's market because it tends to pill up when used alone.

Polyester. Polyester fibers were introduced to carpet-making in the late 1960s. These fibers are soft, durable, and resistant to abrasion. Polyester dyes well, producing a clear, clean color that resists fading. The main detriment to polyester is its resilience; cheap polyester carpets tend to mat in high-traffic areas. However, when polyester is blended with stronger fibers, a more resilient combination results. Polyester is also susceptible to oil-based stains and soil, another hazard in high traffic areas. The most expensive polyesters are made with Trevira fibers, which are shaped in a triangle, the strongest construction component.

Olefin. Olefin fibers are used primarily in commercial carpets, nubby, looped piles called Berbers, and indoor/outdoor carpeting, where resistance to staining and fading is the most important feature. Olefin is comparable to nylon in durability, strength, and wear-resistance. However, olefin is weak in "memory"; it will not bounce back. Olefin carpets are usually constructed in tight, loop pile because of its relatively low resilience. Low-density looped piles in olefin fibers will mat down.

Blends. Blends are combinations of two or more fibers into a single carpet yarn, each fiber lending to the other its dominant characteristics. On the carpet sample label, the dominant fiber within the blend will appear first. Acrylic and nylon fibers often are blended with wool to improve wearability. Herculon's, olefin's, and polypropylene's stain and heat resistance are combined with nylon's strength for heavy-traffic areas where dirt buildup is a problem. There are many blend combinations. Knowing each fiber's characteristics helps to understand the reasoning behind the blend.

Surfaces, Textures, and Patterns. When estimating new carpet for a client, you will inevitably be asked how long the carpet will wear. Since carpet wear is relative for each installation, the answer will depend on several factors. A commercial-grade carpet will have the wearability written in the specification for the carpet, which can be found on the carpet sample folder. The information will state wearability for heavy, medium, and light traffic areas. Heavy-traffic wearability is necessary in theaters, hospitals, and other high-traffic public areas; both density and pile have been designed to withstand this traffic. Medium-traffic carpets would be used in small offices, retail shops, and other areas with moderate foot traffic. Light-traffic carpets would be appropriate to a commercial installation where one to four people work on a daily basis, but stay mostly stationary (e.g. an accounting or computer office). Some commercial bids will require specific guidelines for wearability, yarn weight, and type of installation (see Specifications and Flammability on page 59). For further specific information on wearability, consult the carpet manufacturer's representative directly.

Carpets used in residential settings now have five-to ten-year guarantees printed on the back of the sample. Obviously, any carpet installed in a home with four teenagers, two large dogs, and no outside cleaning service will wear out faster than the same carpet installed in a retired couple's home with no animals.

For many years, both architects and designers have often used a commercial-grade carpet in residential settings. The idea was to install a heavy-duty carpet in a busy home environment for longer wear. Since wear-dating on carpets has been established, the guesswork on durability has been reduced.

Many designers still agree that the best-wearing carpets are either wool or nylon with dense pile in a looped construction. Note: the wearability of the carpet will have a direct bearing on the carpet cost and should be analyzed thoroughly before preparing a carpet estimate.

Regardless of the construction or face fiber, the denser and heavier the carpet pile is, the longer the carpet will wear. The most common styles of carpet piles are level loop, multilevel loop, cut loop, saxony plush, textured plush, frieze, and random sheer.

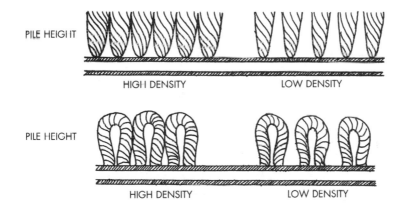

PILE HEIGHT

HIGH DENSITY   LOW DENSITY

PILE HEIGHT

HIGH DENSITY   LOW DENSITY

Level Loop. All carpet starts out looped; from this point, various cuts, designs, and styles are created. Level loop is the simplest style of carpet pile, with pile loops all of equal height and uncut. A level-loop carpet is durable, appropriate for both high-traffic areas and informal room designs. The loop texture is particularly recommended for commercial installations. A tweed coloration or a printed design combined with a level-loop pile will conceal foot marks and soilage. All looped texture carpets show seams more than do cut or plush textured carpets.

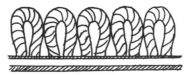

The texture of a Berber-style carpet is a version of a level or multilevel loop; however, the pile is nubby, knobby, and bulky in appearance because the looped pile is fatter. Berber styles are made from every kind of fiber with a wide range of colors, densities, and prices. Like other level-loop carpet, they will show seams.

Multilevel Loop. A multilevel-loop pile carpet has two or three levels of pile forming a random sculptured surface. Patterns can range from large sweeping cloud-like shapes to smaller medallions, classic patterns, and popcorn effects.

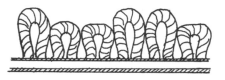

Cut Loop. Cut-loop pile has yarns constructed into islands of high-cut pile and lower loop pile to form a sculptured pattern. This style is available in multiple shades of color and suits more informal settings.

Saxony Plush. This is a one-level cut pile with a pile height of 1/2 inch or less and very dense closely packed yarn. Saxony plush can be made with two-, three- or four-ply yarns to give a dense look that is plain, smooth, and luxurious, giving a formal appearance to a room setting. The pile does show footsteps and shadings.

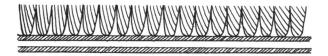

Textured Plush. This style is one-level cut pile with pile heights over 1/2 inch. It has a less dense construction than a saxony plush, and the tip of the yarn is just slightly more open. This carpet style also shows footprints and shading, but it adds a sense of warmth and richness to a less formal room setting.

Frieze. The frieze style of pile is made by tightly twisting cut yarns to give a nubby or pebbly effect. Frieze carpets mask footprints and are rugged enough for heavy-traffic areas in an informal setting.

Random Shear. This style has both cut and uncut loops all at one height, creating a highly textured surface appearance. The random shear style fits both formal and informal settings.

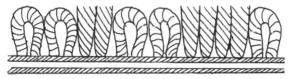

There are multitudes of carpet finishes available on today's market, including fluorocarbon stain repellers and antimicrobial, antifungal, and antiodor compounds that can be applied to the carpet surface. Several of these finishes can be injected into the solution that becomes the synthetic fiber before it is spun. Dyes can also be injected this way; fibers dyed in this method are termed solution-dyed, as the dye becomes part of the fiber. This is a superior dyeing process to piece dyeing, in which the woven or tufted yarn is put into a vat of colored dye.

Carpet Backing. There are two types of carpet backing, primary and secondary, used for every carpet. Carpet backing is the backing on which the yarn is tufted, bonded, or woven regardless of the type of construction. Carpet backing must be dimensionally stable to variations in moisture and temperature to ensure that it lies flat under all conditions. The primary backing locks the fiber loops in place, and over this a secondary backing is bonded to add further strength and stability Both backings are held together with a strong latex glue.

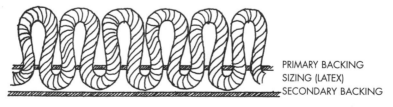

PRIMARY BACKING
SIZING (LATEX)
SECONDARY BACKING

The most common primary backing is Action Back nylon woven or non-woven backing. This is used in 95 percent of commercial complexes where moisture problems exist, such as repeated wet shampooing. It is strong, durable, resists mildew, and is well suited for humid climates.

Another popular primary backing is jute. Jute is a fibrous skin between the bark and stalk of a plant native to India and the Far East. Shredded and spun, jute forms a strong and durable yarn that is used in carpet backing to add strength, weight, and stiffness—making it dimensionally stable. Jute holds adhesives well, but may mildew in very damp conditions. In addition, humidity makes jute backing loose; then, when it dries out, the backing can pull away from tack stripping.

Padding. Carpet padding is a necessary foundation for a carpet installation. Padding has been proven to increase the life of the carpet by 50 percent. Even more than that, padding provides noise and temperature insulation, adds to the feeling of luxury and comfort underfoot, makes vacuuming more effective, and helps retain the texture of the carpet. Independent sources have tested carpet laid over concrete versus carpet laid over a pad. The heat transfer factor of a floor covered by a carpet and separate pad is about one third of what it would be without a pad.

A good thickness for a pad is 1/2 inch. Thin pads can tear, wear down, or disintegrate too quickly. Ultra thick pads can be too soft for comfortable walking; they can cause a feeling of imbalance or dizziness.

Whichever pad you choose, make sure that the warranty is guaranteed for the life of the carpet and has a replacement statement on the warranty. Avoid putting new carpet over an old pad that will wear out before the new carpet, forcing the client at a later date to pull up the carpet to replace the old pad.

Pads are available as felt, foam or sponge rubber, rebonded, and rubber-waffle.

Felt Pads. Felt pads are firmer underfoot than rubber pads. These natural pads are often made by compressing cow's hair with heat and steam. A waffle design is pressed on the top to increase resiliency. Felt pads are always specified by weight, that is, 32 ounces to 86 ounces, with the average weight between 44 and 54 ounces.

Foam or Sponge Rubber Pads. Foam and sponge rubber pads give a degree of firmness underfoot depending on the formulation of the sponge and the shape of the waffle pattern. These pads are made in flat sheets to a thickness of 9/16 inches. Both types have a synthetic-fiber facing material or "skin" laminated to the top side of the pad that the carpet can stretch over for ease in installation.

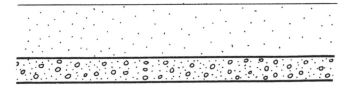

Rebonded Pads. This type of pad is made from scrap pieces of foam or sponge rubber that are bonded together through compression into sheets. Confetti-like foam chunks of different colors and densities appear within the sheets. This pad also has a skin on the top side that the carpet can easily stretch over for ease in installation. This type of pad ranges from 48 ounces to 88 ounces and 1/8-inch thick to 5/8-inch thick, with 1/2 inch average.

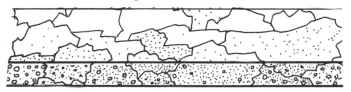

Rubber-Waffle Pads. The waffle pad is made from rubber and has a distinct waffle appearance. This pad is very successful in humid environments, but tends to dry out and disintegrate in dry, desert areas. Rubber-waffle pads come in densities ranging from 40 to 120 ounces; however, the higher densities can make the carpet feel like it is on concrete.

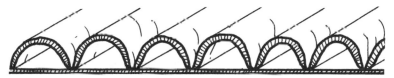

Specifications for Commercial Use. In writing carpet performance guidelines for commercial use, the appropriate tests and standards that are applicable to the installation and federal, state, or local rules should be included in the carpet specification. Carpet specifications can cover a wide range of requirements, depending on the design project. These include construction, pile surface appearance, pile yarn, yarn ply, yarn density, pile weight, pile density, dye method, coloration, dye lot, pile fuzzing and pilling, tuft lock, peel strength of secondary backing, lightfastness, crock-fastness, wet-fastness, AATCC Test Method 134-1979 or electrostatic buildup, flammability, and atmospheric fading. For assistance in writing carpet specifications, contact the manufacturer or the area representative for ratings on each carpet being used for any design project.

Flammability. All carpets offered for sale in the United States must meet the Federal Flammability Standard DOC FF 1-70 (Methenamine Tablet Test ASTM D2859). In addition, many federal and state regulatory agencies require the Flooring Radiant Panel Test (ASTM E648 and NFPA 253) for nonsprinklered corridors and primary exit ways.

Types of Installations. There are three main types of carpet installation. The first type is carpet stretched over carpet padding. This type is primarily used in residential situations. When the carpet is being installed, the outside perimeter of each room has a tacking strip fastened all around the space to be carpeted. This stripping consists of strips of plywood with 1/4-inch tacks sticking straight up to grab or hold the edges of carpet in place after it has been stretched wall to wall. These tacks keep the carpet smooth even after heavy use. To stretch the carpet over the skin of the pad onto the tacking strips, the installer uses a knee kicker for residential jobs and a power stretcher for larger areas. Both devices have gripping teeth at one end to hold the carpet.

The second carpet installation is done with a foam-backed carpet such as a kitchen carpet. This method is mainly used in residential situations. The foam padding and carpet have been fused together in the manufacturing process. The carpet is installed after a clean, flat floor surface is prepared, and a coating of glue is spread on the surface.

The third method is used primarily in commercial spaces. Carpeting is glued directly to the floor without a pad. This method is especially popular where there is traffic from rolling carts. Carpet that is directly glued down must be constructed to withstand this type of heavy use.

MEASURING FOR CARPETING

Carpet Layout or "Map." An important part of carpet planning is the laying out of the complete installation on paper to know exactly where each piece of carpet will go. This carpet layout or "map," whether for one room, a whole house, or a whole office building, is a very important tool that can save money and time. It shows how many square feet of carpet will be used, where seams will show up, and what areas will be covered. With this layout, you can more accurately determine labor charges and even the final aesthetic result.

The way a carpet is laid out can save money A layout that wastes several square feet will cost the client more in extra carpet. On the other hand, if there is not enough carpet, a new order of carpet, with delivery and installation charges, will cost even more.

Time can be saved when the carpet layout is clearly drawn on paper for the installers to review. It will show exactly which direction the carpet will run and where seams will lay, assisting the installers in estimating their time for that job.

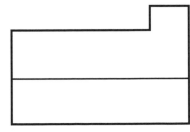 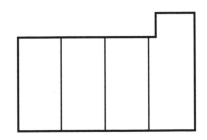

Labor charges can be determined correctly when the layout plan is clear. For example, the plan should show labor-intensive areas such as stairways where carpet has to be cut around each post, and around decorative fireplace hearths or jagged flagstone entries, where installation will take more care and time. Extra labor charges are always charged when there is a carpet coving going up the wall 3 to 4 inches.

Carpet coving is done most often in commercial buildings to keep the wall from looking terrible after years of having a vacuum run along the carpet edge and wall. There are many architectural problems for carpet installation that require special attention, and the layout should clearly show all of them.

The aesthetic beauty of each room can be seen on the carpet layout because the seams will show clearly. This will allow you to decide beforehand to move the long living room seam away from the light of the bay window, for example. Avoid piecing or using multiple seams anywhere. Changing the layout of the carpet on paper is much easier than leaving a major room with an obvious seam that could have been avoided.

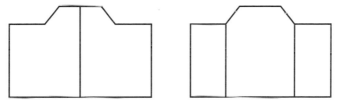

Measuring Floors. Always take your own measurements at the job site. If you have a client who brings figures for a wall-to-wall installation, politely explain that there may be variables that he or she is not aware of that will affect the final costs. Do not order carpet based on the client's figures.

Never assume that walls are parallel and of equal length. In fact, there are no homes or buildings constructed today that are square or that will even match blueprints inch for inch. You should never take measurements from blueprints for anything except a rough guesstimate. Measure the actual area after it is built before placing the final carpet order.

The tools needed for measuring include a metal tape measure of at least 16 to 25 feet (the metal tape can hold its shape in a straight line on the floor and can be pushed along to the end of a wall when there are long spaces to measure) and graph paper and pencils (for drafting a scaled floor layout).

Carefully make a rough sketch of the room, house, or office (this sketch can later be transferred to draft paper). Write down the actual measurements in feet and inches, underlining the inches; i.e., 9⁵. If you use a figure such as 9'5", the feet and inches symbols can easily get mixed up on a rough drawing and mistakes can result.

It is very important to measure each wall separately, noting the measurement of each opening, door, closet, fireplace, stairway, and any other significant features of

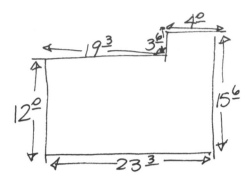

the room. Include every projection, jog, inset, and cove down to approximately 1/2 inch in size. Make sure to measure into each door opening at least one half the way (underneath the closed door). Carpeting at doorways must be seamed to the existing carpeting in other rooms. If only the major areas of the house—living room, dining room, hallways, and master bedroom—are being carpeted, the secondary bedrooms, family room, and/or bathrooms have to have carpet attached or seamed together at the doorways, or trimmed off by a metal strip.

Carpeting that will meet vinyl flooring is usually trimmed off by a metal strip. There are two types of metal strips: one is visible in either a silver or gold finish, and the other is invisible or blind, with the carpet edge turned under to hide the metal strip. When carpeting meets other hard-floor surfaces, transition thresholds can be used, such as wood and marble. The choice of threshold depends on the design; their function is to keep people from tripping when walking from room to room.

It is also advisable to add a safety factor of 2 inches to each room measurement to compensate for the probability of the room's being off-square. Keep in mind that carpet with a jute backing will only stretch 1–2 inches and that carpet with a lock-tuft backing is almost impossible to stretch. It is much safer to be a foot over on a job than to be an inch short. Giving the client one square foot credit is simpler, cheaper, and far more professional than replacing an entire job because your measurements were short. (Waste pieces of carpet can be used for area rugs in utility rooms or bathrooms if the raw edges are bound or serged.) When measurements are short, the first installation has to be pulled up, and a new carpet has to be installed, causing extra materials and labor charges. It is very frustrating to be 6 inches short on a piece of carpet that is 12 by 15 feet long. The correct entire length, 12 by 156 feet has to be ordered again to cover the space, leaving you with an unwanted strip of carpet.

There will always be certain jobs when it is more expedient to call in an experienced carpet installer to measure, lay out, and figure the actual amount of carpet required. This is true when there is an expensive or custom-dyed carpet involved, or in a home or architectural building with unique or irregular angles and shapes. It will also pay to have someone else double-check your figures if you are unsure of your measurements.

Measuring Stairs. The easiest way to measure stairs is as if they were a straight run, going wall to wall. When measuring a flight of stairs in the upstairs hall, include the top step in the hall measurement. Measure the hall to the end of the top step and consider this part of the hall carpet.

Next, measure the first tread and riser from notch to notch. Most stair treads are 10" deep and 8" high.

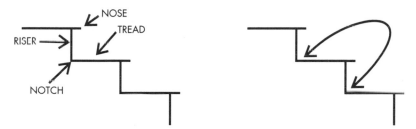

Multiply this amount by the number of stairs. Then measure the width just once (normally stairs are 3 feet wide, but do not assume anything). This figure changes if there are several landings spaced between steps. Quite often carpet waste from other rooms can be used to cover all or part of the steps.

Older or classical homes with curved staircases often use stair runners of oriental or custom design. These runners are installed straight down the center of the staircase, leaving wood on both sides.

ESTIMATING CARPET

Carpet has a grain or a nap that must be followed throughout the installation. If the grain of the carpet goes in the same direction as the predominant traffic pattern, the carpet will wear better. Carpet pieces cannot be turned every which way because the nap will vary wildly.

Carpet Rules

Always: Write feet and inches thus: 9^5, 10^6, 4^0.

Add 2 inches to each measurement for safety.

Run carpet grain in same direction throughout job.

Use same width goods (all 12-foot wide or all 6-foot).

Measure every wall, doorway, cutout, and so forth.

Avoid running seams into a focal point.

Avoid a carpet layout using multiple seams.

Avoid putting new carpet over old pad.

Remember carpet stretches very little, at most 1–2 inches.

Carpet Formula. Ninety-five percent of all carpet manufactured in the United States is 12-feet wide. There are, however, some carpets made in 6-foot widths for kitchens, and there are imported carpets from Belgium that are 13-feet 6-inches wide. Also still in existence is the less popular 15-foot-wide carpet. Never mix different sized carpet goods. The manufacturing process is slightly different in each and the seams, textures, and naps will never match. All examples and work problems will use a carpet width of 12 feet.

Width of cut multiplied by length of cut equals square feet.

PROBLEM ONE

The bedroom on the left gives an ideal example of a simple carpet layout. Think in terms of 12-foot-wide carpet and find the easiest place to lay out the carpet according to its grain or nap with the predominating traffic pattern. This is called a "drop-in" because there are no seams. This example is correct as long as only this room gets new carpet. If the entire house is being carpeted and the grain runs the same way as the example on the right, below, then, unfortunately, all those extra seams would be necessary for that particular room.

The carpet design for the bedroom on the right is wrong for two reasons. First, the traffic into the bedroom goes against the carpet grain. Secondly, the layout has too many seams. Both this layout and the layout on the left use the same amount of carpet, but the room's aesthetics are preserved in the example on the left.

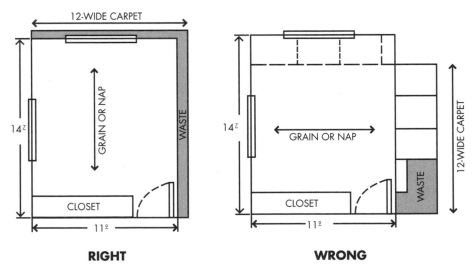

RIGHT
1 cut 12 x 15 = 180 square feet

WRONG
1 cut 12 x 15 = 180 square feet

PROBLEM TWO

There are two layouts shown for the living room below, but only one is correct. The example on the top is correct because it has no seams running into the bay window, there is a minimum of carpet waste, and only two seams show. Two cuts of carpet are used; one is split in half. The living room on the bottom has multiple problems. The seam down the center of the room will be quite noticeable during either day or evening light. In addition, the placement of this layout requires more carpet to be purchased than is necessary.

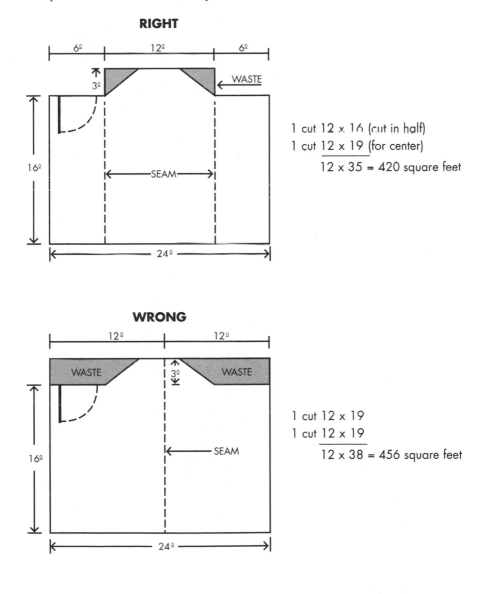

RIGHT

1 cut 12 x 16 (cut in half)
1 cut 12 x 19 (for center)
12 x 35 = 420 square feet

WRONG

1 cut 12 x 19
1 cut 12 x 19
12 x 38 = 456 square feet

PROBLEM THREE

In the example below, you can begin to "see" the carpet layout as you take the measurements and do a rough sketch. When these figures are placed on draft paper (scale 1/4" = 1'), the actual carpet layout is easier to recognize. The stairs have 13 steps, each 3 feet wide; therefore, 59 square feet of carpet are needed. The addition of 2 inches to the measurements helps to round out some of the figures. The entryway and kitchen each have hard flooring. If it is still hard to "see," cut out a piece of carpet from the drafting paper 12 inches wide (to simulate the carpet cut) and place it on your drawing.

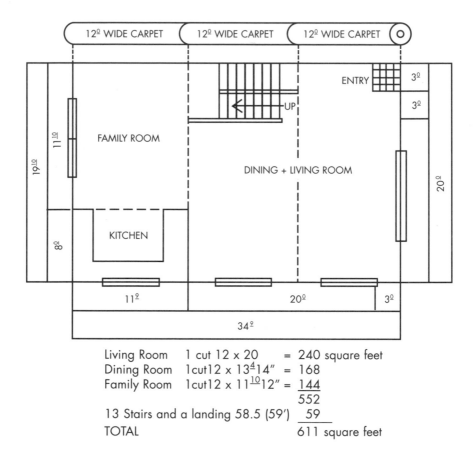

Living Room	1 cut 12 x 20	=	240 square feet
Dining Room	1 cut 12 x 13⁴14"	=	168
Family Room	1 cut 12 x 11¹⁰12"	=	144
			552
13 Stairs and a landing 58.5 (59')			59
TOTAL			611 square feet

COST ESTIMATING

Materials. The materials included in a cost-estimate for a complete carpet installation are usually just carpet and pad. Some installers charge extra for trim strips, but none charges for such materials as tack strips, carpet seam tape, and cutting blades. These materials are used on every installation and are included in the installation figure.

Preparation. There are always other installation issues to consider for each job. Furniture has to be moved out and back by someone. If the installer does it, there is usually an extra charge, especially when a whole houseful of furniture is involved. If there is a large piano to be moved, it may require two men (if it is particularly fragile or valuable, the designer or client needs to budget and make arrangements with a professional moving company). Also, special arrangements may have to be made for large wall units containing heavy objects such as stereo equipment or a large aquarium.

Unless carpeting is going into a new home or building, old carpeting and pads have to be pulled up and discarded, which involves another labor charge. In addition, after this old carpeting has been pulled up, floor repairs may need to be made. Often wooden floors need to have loose boards nailed back in place, and a concrete foundation slab usually needs patching repairs.

The most forgotten and overlooked expense to a new carpet installation is the trimming of interior doors. Many people upgrade their carpet to a thicker, plusher pile; therefore, all interior doors must be trimmed off at the bottom to accommodate the new carpet pile height. It is not a huge expense per door, but it is nevertheless an expense figured into the total job. The carpet installer does not trim doors; a carpenter has to be hired to do this job.

Discussing these added expenses beforehand with your client gives the client correct labor-charge information and avoids surprises at the end of the job. You also enhance your professionalism by advising the client of all labor charges in advance.

The type of installation used will affect the final estimate. For residential installations, extra time may be needed to move furniture, tear up old carpet, and to repair the floor before actual carpet installation can begin. In commercial installations, preparations may be minimal, but carpet coving may slow down the installation process and add to the costs.

Cleanup. The carpet installer's cleanup is limited to removing carpet scraps, tools, and equipment. There will always be small yarn cuttings scattered all over the carpet after the installation, and these need to be vacuumed up. This is not the carpet installer's responsibility; either a cleaning service or the client will need to vacuum up these cuttings. If the client does it, advise him or her that it will usually take two to three vacuumings to get all of the loose cuttings cleaned up.

TIME ESTIMATING

Depending on the size of the job, carpet installation can take from ten days to two weeks or longer depending on the size of the space. After you have called the order into the manufacturer and he or she has verified that the carpet is in stock, the manufacturer will need to set up a ship date based on the company's established trucking routes. This can take a week. Before the carpet and pad are shipped, you need to contact the installer to set up an installation date that coordinates with the client's schedule. The actual carpet installation time can vary depending on the kind of installation. A houseful of carpet can take three to five workdays, depending on the size of the installation team and the competency of the workers. A commercial installation time could range from a few days to several weeks.

SELECTING A CARPET INSTALLER

After the client has decided on the carpet and it has been ordered, you will need to hire a carpet installer. Finding a competent carpet installer takes a little research, but it is well worth the time to find an installer you can count on. Begin by seeking referrals from carpet dealers, carpet manufacturers, other designers, and the Yellow Pages. After you have found two or three promising prospects, set up appointments with them to discuss the kinds of installations they specialize in. Some installers just do a straight installation, but there are a few installers who love to do intricate work with carpet. They can do inserts, borders, and other wonderful installations. These are the people you want on your design team.

During the interview, ask for a list of their labor charges and any extra work expenses that may occur. Request their client references and the names of other designers they work for, and then contact all references. Write down the comments from each reference and add them to the file you have created for this contractor. By developing a habit of creating files for all of your contractors, you will soon have a file cabinet full of possible contractors to call when you need them.

On the first few jobs you assign to them, make sure to visit the job site while the installation is in progress. Make notes on the workmanship and add them to your file. Are the baseboards scuffed or mashed? Are the seams noticeable? Does the person clean up after completing the job? What is the person's attitude toward the client? Carpet installers are generally in great demand, so it pays to foster a good relationship with the ones you wish to work for you.

EXAMPLE OF FINAL CARPETING COSTS

The Palmer family had just completed a major kitchen renovation. The dust and dirt caused by the renovation settled into their old beige carpet and made it look worse. They asked their interior designer to give them an estimate to recarpet their entire house. They chose to upgrade the carpet and padding. Their old carpet will need to be pulled up and removed, plus the furniture will need to be moved out and back. Several meetings were set up to choose a new color and carpet grade.

The Palmers decided on a seafoam color for the new carpet throughout their house, including the bathrooms. The carpet and pad were selected, and the designer measured the entire house and "mapped" it out on graph paper.

Measurements. After all the measuring, drafting, and calculating had been accomplished, the final figures were presented to the clients on a contract. The designer also advised the Palmers that all the doors would need to be slightly trimmed at the bottom because the new carpet would be thicker than the old one. The final estimate would look something like this:

Final Estimates

3000 sq. ft. Camelot-Riviera carpet; color: Taupe @ $3.00 *=	$9,000
3000 sq. ft Rubber padding 3/8" – 5 lbs @ $6.00 =	$900
3000 sq. ft labor and materials @ $.50 =	$1,500
Moving furniture out and back	$100
Removing and carting away old carpet	$75.00
Delivery or trip charge and/or measuring	$20.00
Subtotal	$11,595.00
Tax 7.5% **	$869.62
TOTAL	$12,464.62

* All figures are based on 2001 Phoenix, Arizona prices.

** Each state would calculate tax differently according to their laws. Some states apply tax on newly manufactured products only, not labor. Check your state laws to see what sales and use taxes apply.

Carpet Work Order
SEE ATTACHED FLOOR PLAN—DO NOT PROCEED WITHOUT IT

Designer: _Carol Sampson_   Client: _Mr. + Mrs. Wm. Palmer_

Address: _2705 Camelback Road_   Install Address: _5517 Shadow Lawn Drive_

Scottsdale, Az.   _Scottsdale, Az_

Phone: _(480) 956-5656_   Phone: _(480) 958-6112_

Job Number/P.O. _1075_   Directions/Comments _Don't let_

Installation Date _March 21, 2001_   _friendly dog out, "JAKE."_

Name of Installer _John Harrison Installations_

INSTALLATION PREPARATION:

Measure Job?	Yes ✓	No ____	Price $20.00
Furniture to be moved?	Yes ✓	No ____	Price 100.00
Old carpet to be removed?	Yes ✓	No ____	Price 75.00
Floor patching w/Fixall?	Yes ____	No ✓	Price ____
Nail loose wood flooring?	Yes ____	No ✓	Price ____
Delivery charge?	Yes ____	No ✓	Price ____

THRESHOLD TRIM:

Wood	Feet ____	Yes ____	No ____	Price ____
Marble	Feet ____	Yes ____	No ____	Price ____
Corian — 2	Feet _3'_	Yes ✓	No ____	Price -0-
Miscellaneous	Feet ____	Yes ____	No ____	Price ____

DOORWAY TRIM STRIP:

Blind/Invisible	Feet _16_	Yes ✓	No ____	Price -0-
Gold Aluminum	Feet ____	Yes ____	No ____	Price ____
Silver Aluminum	Feet ____	Yes ____	No ____	Price ____

WALL PROTECTION:

Vinyl Base	Linear Feet ____	Yes ____	No ____	Price ____
Color ____				
Carpet Coving	Linear Feet ____	Yes ____	No ____	Price ____
Height ____				
Trim Strip	Linear Feet ____	Yes ____	No ____	Price ____

Carpet Co.   Padding Supplier _Superior_

Manufacturer _Camelot_   Manufacturer _ABC_

Carpet Name/# _Riviera_   Weight _5 lb._

Color _Taupe_   Thickness _3/8 "_

Content _100% Nylon_   Content _Foam_

Total Square Feet _3,000_   Total Square Feet _3000_

DOOR TRIMMING AFTER INSTALLATION:

Number of Doors _15_   Date/Time _4-2-2001_   Price per Door $7.50

CLEAN UP:

Client ✓   Janitorial ____   Date/Time ____   Price ____

Carpet Work Order
SEE ATTACHED FLOOR PLAN—DO NOT PROCEED WITHOUT IT

Designer: _____   Client: _____

Address: _____   Install Address: _____

_____   _____

_____   _____

Phone: _____   Phone: _____

Job Number/P.O. _____   Directions/Comments _____

Installation Date _____   _____

Name of Installer _____   _____

INSTALLATION PREPARATION:

Measure Job?	Yes____	No____	Price_____
Furniture to be moved?	Yes____	No____	Price_____
Old carpet to be removed?	Yes____	No____	Price_____
Floor patching w/Fixall?	Yes____	No____	Price_____
Nail loose wood flooring?	Yes____	No____	Price_____
Delivery charge?	Yes____	No____	Price_____

THRESHOLD TRIM:

Wood	Feet_____	Yes___	No____	Price_____
Marble	Feet_____	Yes____	No____	Price_____
Corian	Feet_____	Yes____	No____	Price_____
Miscellaneous	Feet_____	Yes____	No____	Price_____

DOORWAY TRIM STRIP:

Blind/Invisible	Feet_____	Yes____	No____	Price_____
Gold Aluminum	Feet_____	Yes____	No____	Price_____
Silver Aluminum	Feet_____	Yes____	No____	Price_____

WALL PROTECTION:

Vinyl Base	Linear Feet_____	Yes____	No____	Price_____
Color _____				
Carpet Coving	Linear Feet_____	Yes____	No____	Price_____
Height _____				
Trim Strip	Linear Feet_____	Yes____	No____	Price_____

Carpet Co. _____   Padding Supplier _____

Manufacturer _____   Manufacturer _____

Carpet Name/# _____   Weight _____

Color _____   Thickness _____

Content _____   Content _____

Total Square Feet _____   Total Square Feet _____

DOOR TRIMMING AFTER INSTALLATION:

Number of Doors_____   Date/Time____   Price per Door_____

CLEAN UP:

Client_____   Janitorial_____   Date/Time____   Price_____

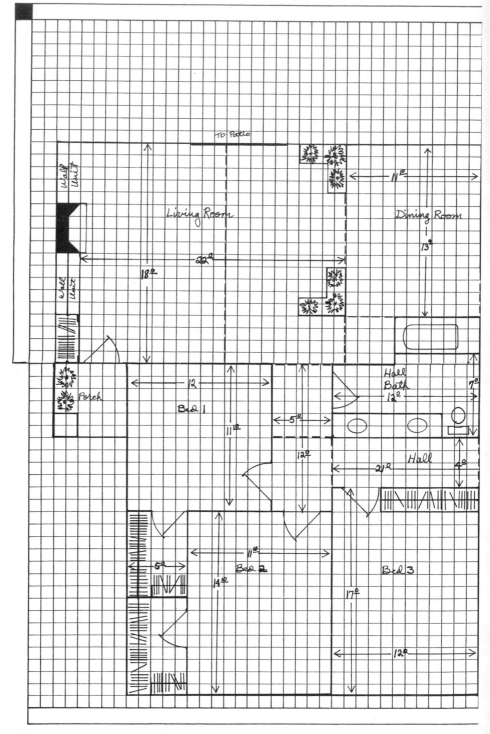

FLOOR PLAN

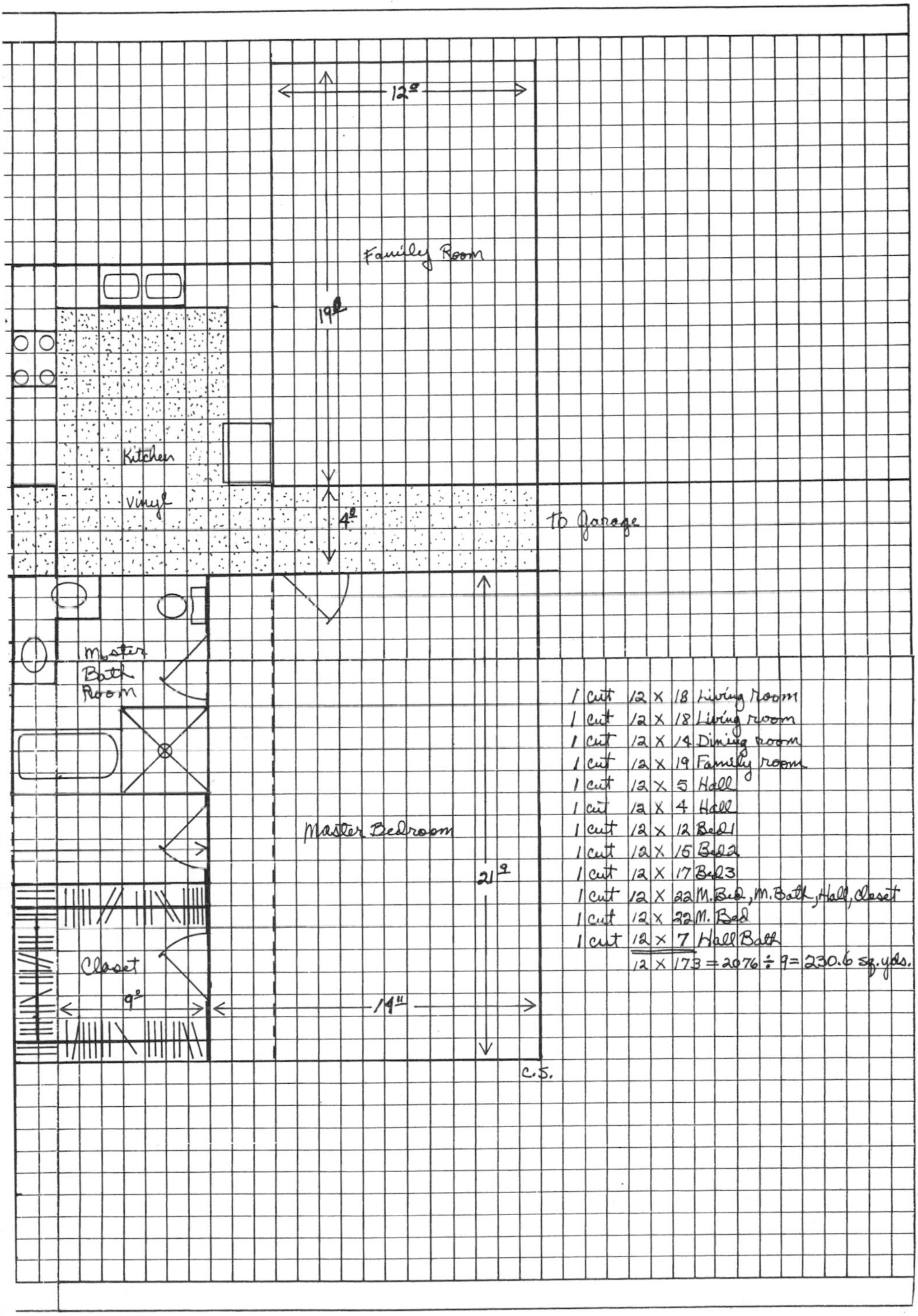

Family Room

12⁸

19²

Kitchen

vinyl

4²

to Garage

Master Bath Room

Master Bedroom

21²

Closet

9⁸

19"

c.s.

1 cut 12 × 18 Living room
1 cut 12 × 18 Living room
1 cut 12 × 14 Dining room
1 cut 12 × 19 Family room
1 cut 12 × 5 Hall
1 cut 12 × 4 Hall
1 cut 12 × 12 Bed 1
1 cut 12 × 15 Bed 2
1 cut 12 × 17 Bed 3
1 cut 12 × 22 M. Bed, M. Bath, Hall, Closet
1 cut 12 × 22 M. Bed
1 cut 12 × 7 Hall Bath
12 × 173 = 2076 ÷ 9 = 230.6 sq. yds.

Chapter Four
DRAPERY

Draperies trimmed
with metal and glass
beads, tied back
with a camel tie.

Draperies have a long and well-documented history. Illustrated manuscripts from the Middle Ages depict drapery treatments of those times, and many old paintings (approximately 200 A. D.) show multilayered and elaborately defined draperies. In the wealthier households, draperies sometimes had festoons, cascading fabrics, fringes, tassels, rope tiebacks, and even a plume of feathers or two. The peasants of the Middle Ages covered their windows with oiled paper or linen, animal skins, and wood shutters.

During the Middle Ages, in the colder climates of Europe, windows were narrow slits that allowed smoke from the fires to escape while letting in fresh air. These windows also helped light the room and permitted glimpses of the world outside.

From the fifteenth to the seventeenth centuries, architectural changes in buildings, brought on by the influence of the Italian Renaissance, caused windows to become larger, allowing more light into the interior. Gradually, as windows became taller and wider to allow better views of the surrounding landscape, heavy, thick, woolen draperies were added to keep out cold drafts. These floor-length draperies were hung straight rather than tied back so they could be easily drawn across the window. Draperies were also used to partition spaces within larger rooms and around the beds.

In warmer climates, draperies were made of lightweight fabrics like cotton, linen, and silk. These were intended more to provide privacy than to control interior temperatures.

Across Europe, the Renaissance period introduced a renewed reverence for the classical styles of Athens. New interpretations of classical artistry affected window treatments. The fabrics draping the windows were solid, neutral tones trimmed down the front edge and hem of the drapery. Quite often fringe was the preferred decorative treatment at the valance. Valances were hung from a wooden frame trimmed with a crown molding.

During the reigns of Louis XIII, Louis XIV, Louis XV, and Louis XVI (1610–1790) draperies reached a zenith in decorative layer and embellishment. Windows were as beautifully swathed as the women of the royal French court. This period saw draperies of fine woven fabrics trimmed with gold or silver threads, multicolored fringes, classical braids, heavy tassels, and tricolored cording. Elaborate cornices were contoured and outlined with trims. Softer valances had fabrics molded to form swags, festoons, jabots, poufs, and bows. Both top treatments—soft valances or cornices, were ornamented with finials, shells, rosettes, feathers, and fringes—and rich effects were achieved by layering several pairs of draperies. State beds of kings and queens in many countries were particularly elaborate because of the custom of royalty receiving special guests before rising. In fact, special ceremonies surrounded the awakening and dressing of his royal highness, King Louis XIV making his bedchamber as important a room as the throne room in state affairs.

During the Directoire period in France (1795–99), military motifs were intro-

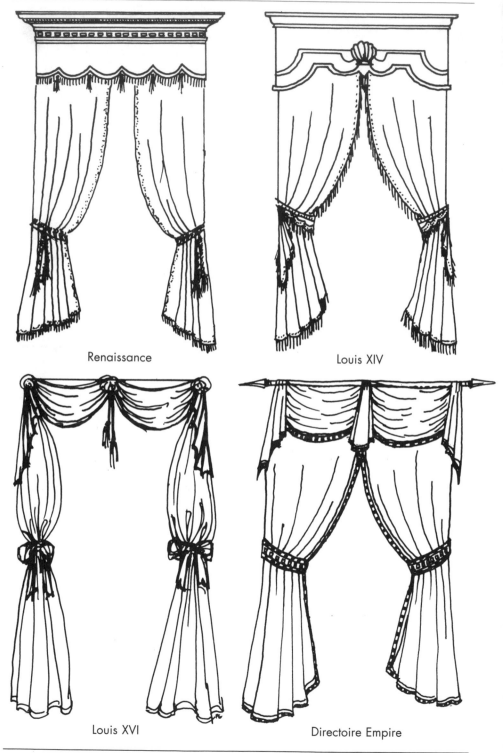

Renaissance

Louis XIV

Louis XVI

Directoire Empire

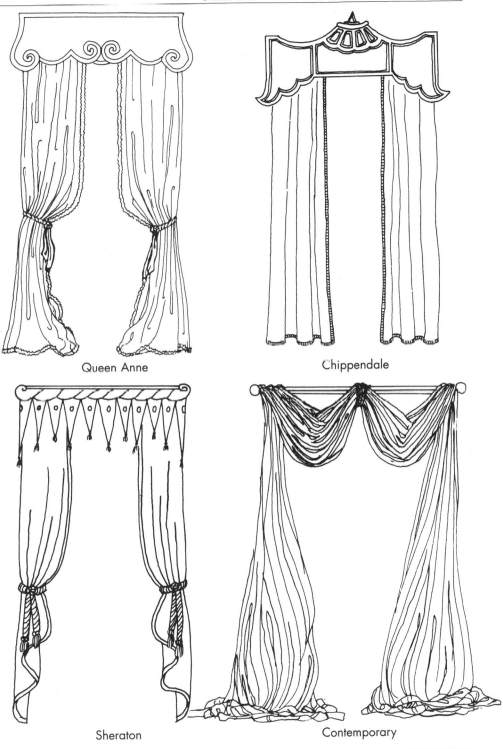

Queen Anne

Chippendale

Sheraton

Contemporary

duced in window treatments and continued into the Empire period, during the reign of Napoleon (1804–15). Window treatments of the time reflected his tastes at home; Egyptian motifs and allegorical symbols of Rome and Greece were used, including the popular spear motif that is still used today.

At the beginning of the eighteenth century, under the rule of Queen Anne, the English slightly simplified interiors. Curvilinear shapes were applied to furniture and window cornices and valances alike. In addition, oriental designs were introduced as a result of the trade with China. As this century progressed, a strong oriental influence became identified with the Chippendale period.

During the later 1700s, two cabinetmakers, Sheraton and Adam, influenced furniture design so strongly that their styles spilled over into all aspects of interior design, including drapery treatments. Although their designs were English in origin, both men had been influenced by English and French styles, which they blended together for a graceful, simplified look using restraint and refinement in the swags, valances, and trims.

Just before the Industrial Revolution took off in the late eighteenth century, during the Regency period in England and the Empire period in France, Athens and Rome again influenced the design of furniture and draperies, and classical designs abounded. American designs closely followed the continental period styles with minor variations.

TODAY'S DRAPERY FUNCTIONS

Drapery treatments today have six functions: to provide privacy, energy conservation, light control, view enhancement, noise control, and decoration. Draperies used as bed canopies, at doorways, and as wallcoverings are strictly design elements. These treatments are measured and estimated in the same manner as window drapery treatments.

Privacy is the major reason for treating windows. The amount of privacy needed depends on the window location. Privacy will be a factor when the window faces a sidewalk or is directly facing a neighbor's window. Good drapery coverage is especially critical in bedrooms and bathrooms.

Energy conservation has become an extremely important factor in interiors. Duopane windows help immensely to conserve inside temperature; however many homes older than ten years do not have these windows. Regional climates will also affect drapery treatments. Window dressings designed for the blistering Southwest will obviously differ from those designed for Los Angeles or the colder Northeast area. Layering window treatments provides insulation in both hot and cold climates.

Window direction plays a major role in light control. Windows facing south receive more light and heat during the summer than other windows; as a result, these windows require special and/or multilayered treatments. These windows allow the most sun to penetrate an interior, which can cause interior fabrics, carpets, and furnishings to fade. If the bedroom windows face east, the rising sun will

Country French swags and jabots.

awaken the occupants. West-facing windows will show off beautiful sunsets; however, when these windows are in the kitchen, the glare can interfere with dinner preparations requiring perhaps a multilayered treatment. Northern window exposures have the most even light and can be treated without worrying about the sun's damaging rays. Drapery treatments can also become a design element when used to add light to a room that is too dark or to dim a room that is too light.

Layering window treatments for insulation helps to control noise as well as temperature. Outside traffic and close neighbors present common noise problems. Fabrics and woods absorb sounds, reducing noise both inside and outside.

Drapery panels, in a rich fabric, hung from decorative iron rods and rings.

Windows with views overlooking shorelines, mountains, valleys, and city sky-lines usually come with high price tags, so minimal window treatments are welcome. Framing such windows with soft fabrics reduces the harsh, straight lines of the window frames. There are also a fair share of windows that look out on walls, unattractive buildings, freeways, and other unsightly views. These windows need total coverage.

In designing drapery treatments, you must take all these elements into consideration and at the same time come up with a design that adds sparkle, elegance, and uniqueness to the bare window opening. Good design can visually disguise flaws while enhancing the window function and the interior of the room.

DRAPERY BASICS

When estimating for draperies, it is important to have an understanding of the basic construction and function of draperies. Because 95 percent of draperies are used for windows, it is also helpful to be familiar with the various window styles and functions available.

Construction Basics. A drapery treatment can be a simple single window covering, or it can have many layers and parts. Every drapery has a top header, pins to attach to the rod, a bottom hem, corner hem weights, and two side seams. In addition, other layers can be added to the drapery, such as linings, decorative trims, tiebacks, and valances.

Drapery Materials. Many different kinds of fabrics are used for drapery treatments. Most designers are required to take a course in textiles to learn the best fabrics for any design project. The fiber contents, designs, and prices of fabrics are constantly changing. Today's designers can select fabrics manufactured in the United States, Japan, or Europe. Beautiful cotton prints come from England, Holland, France, and Belgium. Many laces are made in England, Belgium, and Switzerland. Lining fabrics made in the United States can be plain cottons or blackouts made with an aluminum or rubberized coating applied to the cotton. Other fiber selections include silks; synthetics of rayon, nylon, acetate, polyester; and blends. Drapery fabric prices range from the cheapest at six dollars per yard to as high as ninety-six dollars per yard with the average falling in the twenty-to-fifty-dollar range. Most fabrics are woven in 48- and 54-inch widths.

Drapery Accessories. In addition to the basic elements, draperies have different accessories used for different practical and/or purely decorative purposes. Drapery liners, valances, swags and jabots, cornices, lambrequins and cantonnieres, tiebacks, trims, and braids are all different drapery accessories that can be used separately or in combination for different effects.

Drapery Liners. Drapery linings are used to protect draperies, adding to their durability and longevity; provide added insulation in colder climates; and block sunlight that can damage or fade fabrics and disturb sleeping occupants. Lining can be used to give weight to lighter, thinner fabrics, helping them hang better. Drapery linings can make the outside view of windows look uniform. Lining materials include cotton, sateen, polyesters, and milium.

Most formal draperies are lined, especially those made with silk. A lining protects the silk from the sun, which will fade the color and break down the natural proteins of the silk threads. Silk draperies and their linings should have a pillow slip hemline (no overlapping fabric) with no exposed folded seams that the sunlight can damage.

Thermal lining acts as an insulator, doubling the layers of fabric between the room rature outside. One type of thermal lining is called interlining. This lining has the feel of flannel and is sewn between the exterior fabric and the regular lining. Interlining is mostly used in cold climates, especially in Europe, because of the extra insulaation value. In addition, the added layer of interlining makes some fabrics look more luxurious.

Blackout lining is used by people who sleep during the day and by the hotel industry. It is made from a cotton or linen face fabric that is laminated to an aluminum or rubber backing. The third kind has a suedelike finish face fabric and is commonly used in hotels. This lining should be sewn with the liner or cotton side facing outward. If left exposed, the fuzzy side will collect dust and the drapery will cling to it, ruining the drape of the fabric.

The drapery fabric and lining you select must be compatible. A cotton print or lace drapery would work well with a light lining. A lightweight, textured fabric would not work well with a heavy blackout lining. When a colored lining is used, expect a color change on the right side of the drapery because penetrating sunlight will cast the liner color onto the front drapery. The color of the interior drapery can also be affected by the penetration of daylight through the lining and drapery fabric, causing a "yellow or gray" tone to come through to the face fabric. Test fabric and lining together against the light to determine their compatibility before committing to the expense of fabrication.

Valances. A valance is a soft, horizontal treatment made entirely of fabrics mounted at the top of draperies. The valance primarily serves the function of camouflaging drapery headers or top double hem of drape, rods, and hardware while adding a decorative element.

Valances can be attached to a mounting board with Velcro, staples, or tacks, or hung on a rod depending on the style of heading used. Those that are attached with Velcro can be easily removed for cleaning. In addition, the Velcro does less damage to the fabric than staples or tacks.

Valance headings can be pleated, shirred, or gathered—or pleated at various intervals and flat in others. The valance style, whichever is selected, must coordinate with the style of the drapery. Pleated, shirred, and gathered valances are often miniatures of the drapery below.

To determine the correct length of any valance, evaluate the scale of both the window and room. In rooms with eight-foot ceilings, for example, valances look best if they are 18 to 22 inches deep. A larger, deeper valance would dwarf the appearance of the room.

Valances need to be lined (preferably self-lined) so that they have a finished appearance when seen from the outside. The back sides of fabrics, particularly patterned ones, are very unattractive. Valances using patterned fabrics should be self-lined, since seam shadows of a patterned fabric often show through a solid white or colored lining.

Swags and Jabots. Swags are fabrics festooned between two points; a jabot is a valance end piece of fabric draped down in a folded S-shaped design. Swags and jabots can be used in every possible combination of fabrics and styles. Also called festoons, swags can be used singly, doubly, in multiples, alone, or with jabots. Depending on the weight of the fabric, they can be constructed from either the straight (direction of weave) or the bias (diagonal of weave) of a fabric.

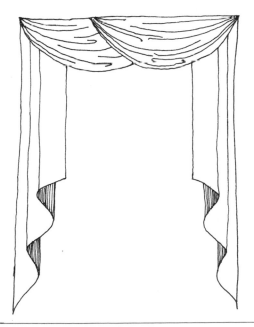

Jabots, also known as cascades because of their stair-step design, can be self-lined, or lined with a decorative contrasting print or strip, or a solid fabric. They can be trimmed with braids or fringes.

The length of jabots can vary from one-third the size of the window to floor length, in which case they substitute for drapery. Depending on the design, jabots can be installed under swags or on top of swags.

Estimating fabric yardage for swags is difficult because of the weight of the fabric and its ability to drape in any treatment. You will have to consult your drapery workroom for an accurate yardage estimate from your finished width and length measurements, and from the type of fabric specified.

Cornices. A cornice is a firm, horizontal, boxlike structure wall-mounted at the top of draperies. As with a valance, its main purpose is to camouflage drapery headers, rods, and other hardware while adding a decorative element. Cornices are usually constructed from a wooden frame of 1/2-inch quality plywood, which is then painted, stained, padded, and/or upholstered (polyester fiberfill is used for padding). When the cornice is upholstered in fabric, the inside needs to be finished off with lining fabric and gimp glued over the top of staples.

Cornices can be trimmed with welts, gimps, braids, border fabrics, nail heads, or moldings. A welt is a cord covered in the cornice fabric or a contrasting fabric. Gimps are woven flat cords constructed in an S-shaped pattern. They come in all different colors and are used on drapery treatments and upholstery pieces to cover glue or staples.

Lambrequins/Cantonnieres. These accessories are very similar and some workrooms confuse these terms, so make sure they understand which one you want. A lambrequin is a four-sided cornice completely surrounding a window, while a cantonniere is a three-sided shaped or straight cornice going across the top of the window and down both sides to the floor. Both can be painted, stained, wallpapered, padded, or upholstered. Functionally, both lambrequins and cantonnieres can overcome erratic window architecture by tying together odd sizes and shapes; they offer handsome solutions to problem windows.

Since lambrequins and cantonnieres are usually covered in flat fabrics without fullness, it is easy to estimate their yardage. First, measure from top to bottom with one width of fabric across (48 or 54 inches off the bolt). The sides of most lambrequins/cantonnieres are only 22 inches or less, so fabric can be split in half to fit each side. The top center of the frame would need one or more widths of fabric the length of the top frame only. For example, using a 54-inch fabric, a 94-inch-wide cantonniere would need one long width of fabric split in half for each side and one short width for the middle top of the cantonniere using a 54-inch fabric.

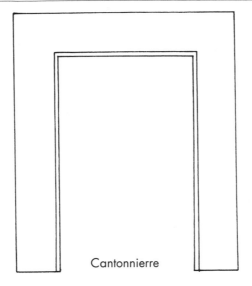

Cantonnierre

Tiebacks. Tiebacks are pieces of decorative fabrics, cords, braids, or hardware designed to hold drapery open at the window and also to add a finishing embellishment. Fabric tiebacks can be tailored, single- or double-ruffled, and corded or braided in styles to coordinate with the drapery treatment.

Tiebacks can usually be made from scrap fabric left over from the making of the drapery or by adding an extra half yard of fabric to the drapery estimate. Most tiebacks should be 2 to 4 inches wide and as long as half the finished width of the treatment. For ruffled tiebacks, use the total finished width to get double fullness into the tieback.

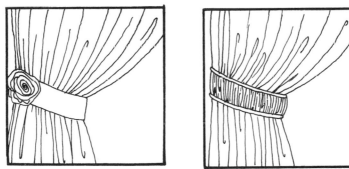

Trims and Braids. Trims and braids have long been rich embellishments for draperies, valances, cornices, lambrequins, cantonnieres, and tiebacks. There are a multitude of trims available on today's market in a variety of sizes, colors, and materials, including rayon, silk, and cotton. Styles of trims include cut, loop, corded, bell, ball, and braid and tassel. Several styles are quite often combined. In addition, the cut and loop fringes have specific style names, such as bouclé, moss, chain, scallop, and bullion. Tassel fringes have a heading of simple or elaborate woven braids; the tassels themselves can be looped or cut, hanging in a straight row or in alternating heights. Custom-colored trims are available but must be ordered in a minimum amount of yardage and an extra fee will be charged to customize the trim. Most trims are fabricated by hand and can be very expensive.

There are several ways of attaching trims, but the most common is using a special fabric glue. The most time-consuming method, hand sewing, is used for attaching complicated trims.

WINDOW FUNCTIONS

Since most draperies hang at windows, it is important to have an understanding of the different window styles and their functions when measuring and estimating draperies for them. The main functions of windows are still, as in the past, to provide ventilation and light. Although fires are no longer built in the center of rooms, cross-ventilation is a major factor in the placement of windows in home construction today.

Over the centuries, windows have gotten larger to allow in more light and to open up the outside view. Today's homes tend to have a more intimate relationship between the exterior and interior spaces. The outside can be visually brought into the interior spaces through the use of sliding patio windows, bay windows, arched windows, and ceiling-height windows (often these windows can prove to be a design challenge for drapery treatments and estimating).

WINDOW STYLES

In the past fifteen years, windows have been getting much more attention both in the construction industry as well as in the interior design field. There are two categories of windows, basic and unique, and within these categories there are fixed windows, architecturally designed for light and views, and movable windows, additionally used for ventilation. Today's windows can be a combination of fixed and movable. In addition, duo-panes and tints are often used to provide better energy conservation without sacrificing a view. The majority of fixed or movable windows now come in standardized sizes and in systems of prefabricated units. This development has lowered initial construction costs, installation costs, and remodeling replacement costs for both home and commercial uses.

Many basic and unique windows have technical considerations inherent to their particular window structure. It is important for the designer, the drapery workroom, and the installer each to understand the various window styles and the specific conditions that apply to installing draperies on them.

Basic Windows. Basic window styles include double-hung, picture, casement, awning, ranch, jalousie, sliding glass doors, and window wall.

Double-Hung. The most common style of window is the double-hung window. This window has two sashes to the frame, and both slide vertically. Weights or springs hold the sashes in place when they are opened either on the top or bottom.

For double-hung windows, drapery should be installed on the adjacent walls instead of on the sash or wooden frame. This will allow the window to be opened and closed without catching or tangling the draperies in the process.

Picture. The picture window has one fixed piece of glass in the center and two horizontal sliding or double-hung windows placed at either side for ventilation. This style has the same advantages as a double-hung window with the added feature of a large center glass for a greater view. Drapery for picture windows should be installed off the window frame to allow for the opening and closing of the side windows.

Casement. Casement windows are hinged on one side and swing inside or outside like doors to direct or control the amount of air allowed into the room. They are equipped with a crank or a similar piece of hardware for easy opening and closing. However, these cranks can get tangled with the interior drapery, especially if there is a breeze. Casement windows can also be an outside hazard to people and plants. Sheer short draperies can be mounted directly onto the wooden casement frames or longer draperies can be hung on the adjacent walls to pull across the entire window.

Awning. Awning windows have wide horizontal sashes, hinged at the top, that swing outward at an angle. They allow cooling breezes to enter the room, even during rain. A fixed pane above an awning window allows for a larger view and floor-level ventilation. Some awning windows swing into the room and can cause problems with drapery treatments. Awning windows require drapery to be hung on adjacent walls away from the mechanical opening windows or a Roman-shade type of design can be used to move the window treatment up and out of the way

Ranch. Ranch windows, like picture windows, have a fixed pane of glass and one or two horizontal sliding sashes. However, they are usually set 5 feet or higher off the floor. They are constructed to allow for ventilation and total privacy and are most commonly found in bathrooms and bedrooms. Often this window style presents a design challenge; long draperies look out of proportion to the window and shorter draperies tend to visually float in the air. Roman shades or other custom shades used inside the window, as well as sheer fabrics used outside the window are good solutions for this problem.

Jalousie. Jalousie windows use the same principle as awning windows except that they have multiple narrow strips of glass without a sash or frame. They give precise ventilation control; however, they are not as weatherproof as awning windows, they can interfere with a view, and they are difficult to clean. The glass strips can

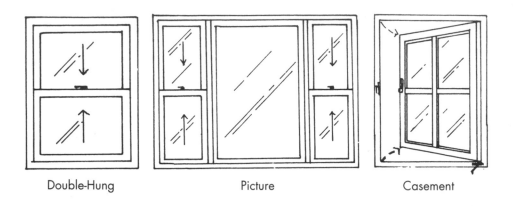

Double-Hung   Picture   Casement

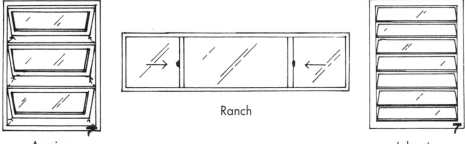

Awning   Ranch   Jalousie

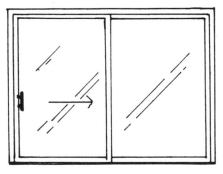

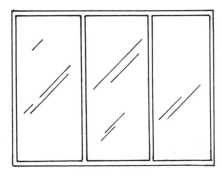

Sliding Glass Doors   Window Wall

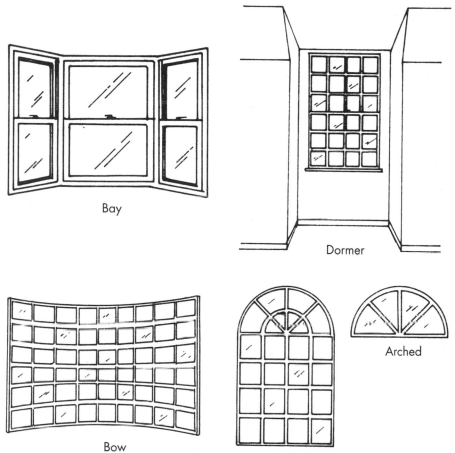

Bay

Dormer

Bow

Arched

Arched

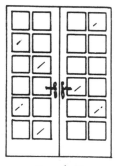

Clerestories

French Doors

interfere with longer draperies and inhibit the placement of hardware. The best way to treat these windows is with shades or wall-hung draperies pulled across the entire window away from the glass.

Sliding Glass Doors. Sliding glass doors have one or more movable glass doors and one or more stationary pieces of glass. This window usually gives access to an exterior patio, garden area, or deck. Draperies covering a sliding door need to be made as a one-way draw panel, with the direction of the draw carefully specified.

Window Wall. Window walls are a group of floor-to-ceiling windows covering a large expanse to form a window or glass wall. A window wall can be used at various levels, serve different purposes, and become an architectural statement of design. Drapery treatments are unrestricted and open to simple or elaborate designs because there are no window mechanisms to interfere.

Unique Windows. Unique window styles include bay dormer, bow, arched, clerestory and French doors.

Bay. The bay window is a projection of the wall beyond the house with three or more windows set at an angle to each other. This window configuration offers endless design possibilities. Draperies for bay windows need to have returns at each inside corner and the rods need to be slightly longer so they can overlap at the corners. The drapery installer needs to be consulted for a perfect drapery fit for every bay window treatment. Designs of these window treatments can be simple individual window coverings or elaborate multilayered treatments depending on the budget and design.

Dormer. The dormer window is a small window projecting from the top story of a house that breaks the surface of the sloping roof, creating an alcovelike extension of the interior room. This window can be treated in many wonderful ways, from a simple individual treatment to elaborate multilayered treatments, depending on the design and budget.

Bow. A bow window is a circular bay or curved window, usually with fixed panes. Special drapery rods need to be adjusted to fit the curve.

Arched. An arched or half-circle window can be in a solitary position or on top of stationary or movable windows with multiple panes. This window also needs special attention to get the correct curvature for both drapery and rod. Usually arched windows are treated with a gathered fabric on a curved rod.

Clerestory. Clerestory windows are placed at the roof of a house or high in a wall. Often there is a sloping angle to the window Intended to illuminate and sometimes ventilate while retaining privacy for the occupants, these windows also make a strong architectural statement. Some clerestory windows receive drapery; in this case, the level of the top slope is important to consider to get the hems and headers at the correct angle when using a totally covered window treatment.

French Doors. French doors have six to twelve panes of fixed glass within a door frame. One or two French doors are often placed at an exit onto a patio or deck. Drapery and rods for French doors are either mounted on the doors or far enough off the door frame to keep the draperies from tangling when the doors are opened and closed.

HOW TO MEASURE FOR DRAPERIES

Accurate measuring is vital for estimating yardage for the fabrication of any drapery treatment. A quick sketch of the window on a piece of paper creates a window "map" for recording measurements and for creating multiple design choices for the window. Many more options are open for discussion when several approaches are taken for a window treatment.

Measurements need to be accurate enough to figure fabric yardage, labor, hardware, and installation. (Always measure and record your measurements in inches to avoid errors in your calculations later.) A follow-up remeasure can be made by the drapery installer to guarantee final accuracy and spell out any technical details needed before any yardage is ordered.

For measuring, always use a 16- to 25-foot-long steel tape measure with a 3/4-inch-wide blade. This type of measuring tape will remain stiff as it is pushed up a wall or along a sill.

First, measure the window opening, the finished width, and the finished length. The window opening measurement is necessary to figure the amount of stacking (the amount of space the drapery occupies on the wall when it is open, also called stack back). The finished width and finished length are the width and length measurements of the finished drapery as it will hang closed at the window. From these measurements the allowances for what is hidden from view—returns and overlaps, stacking, hems and headers, fullness, and pattern matching—can be calculated.

You will need inside window measurements for estimating yardage for draperies hanging inside the window frame—curtains, Roman shades, pleated shades, mini-

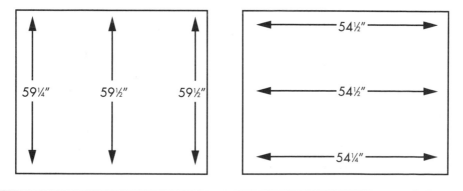

blinds, and roll shades. Because almost every window will be slightly off-square, for tightfitting treatments such as shades, take inside measurements in three places for both width and length.

To be sure that the shade has enough clearance to open and close, subtract 1/4 inch from your narrowest measurement and use this figure as your finished width. A final measurement would look like this:

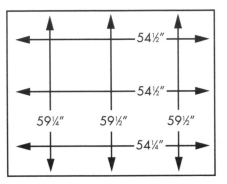

Seventy-five percent of all drapery treatments will require measurements from outside of the window. Hanging traverse draperies can hang on the window frame or can be pulled back onto the walls on either side of the window. The exact position depends on the window type, the drapery style, and the amount of wall space to be covered.

Drapery Allowances. There are different options that need fabric allowances and these need to be figured into the drapery calculation. The allowances are for returns and overlaps, stacking, hems and headers, fullness, and pattern matching. Nearly all drapery designs will require at least one of these allowances.

Returns and Overlaps. Most draperies have returns and overlaps. A return is the space from the rod face back to the wall. Some rods turn toward the wall and some do not. Regardless of the type of rod used, the drapery must have a return to be able to swing toward the wall for privacy, to keep out light, and to complete the side of the drapery.

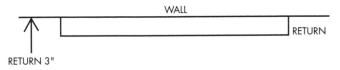

Returns are usually 3 to 3 1/2 inches deep. Every time another rod or layer of drapery is added to a treatment, a longer return is needed to get past the first rod and drapery. Not only is extra depth needed, but extra wall width is needed as well.

Overlaps are the part of the drapery at the center that the master carrier of a tra-

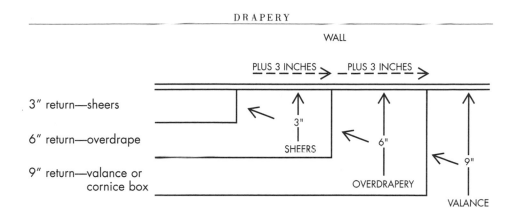

verse rod pulls together and overlaps when draperies are closed. These overlaps are usually 3 inches on each side. They are designed to close out light, give privacy and finish off the face of the drapery.

Returns and overlaps generally total 12 inches of extra width on drapery measurements. They are designated by writing "R. & O." when measuring or filling out a work order.

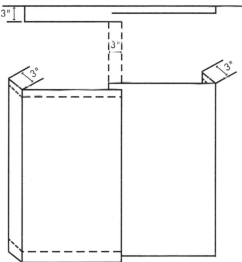

Stacking. Stacking is the amount of space the draperies occupy on the wall when they are open. Drapery stacking will figure into most treatments to allow the most light into the room—and to permit the best view out. Stacking is usually one third the width of the glass area. If bulky fabric is being used, add to this allowance an extra inch for each width of fabric being used. For a two-way draw treatment, place half the stacking amount on either side of the glass. For a one-way draw treatment, place the entire stacking on one side of the glass.

To determine the stacking area for windows, measure the glass width, divide by 3, and add 12 inches for returns and overlap. (For stacking fractions .4 and under round down, .5 and over round up. The difference can be made up in the pleating.) For example, if the glass is 60 inches, divide by 3 to get 20 inches, then add 12 inches for returns and overlap to get a 32-inch stacking area. Add stacking width to glass width for the total finished rod width: 92 inches. Total finished rod width has to be determined before a drapery estimate can be started.

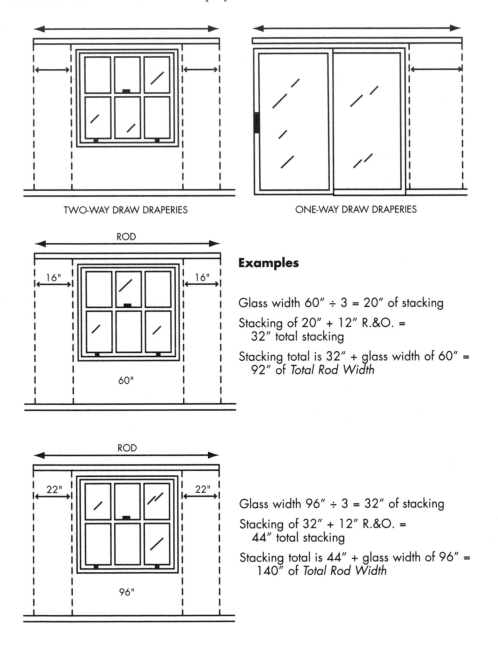

TWO-WAY DRAW DRAPERIES

ONE-WAY DRAW DRAPERIES

ROD

16" 16"

60"

Examples

Glass width 60" ÷ 3 = 20" of stacking

Stacking of 20" + 12" R.&O. = 32" total stacking

Stacking total is 32" + glass width of 60" = 92" of *Total Rod Width*

ROD

22" 22"

96"

Glass width 96" ÷ 3 = 32" of stacking

Stacking of 32" + 12" R.&O. = 44" total stacking

Stacking total is 44" + glass width of 96" = 140" of *Total Rod Width*

Stacking Chart. Use the following chart to estimate stacking allowances, rod measurements, and bracket placement for basic window treatments.

STACKING CHART					
Formula Glass width ÷ 3 + 12 inches return and overlap = total stacking Stacking + glass size = rod measurement and drapery coverage					
Glass Size	Plus Return & Overlap	Stacking* Area	Stacking & Glass Size	Rod Measurement & Drapery Width Coverage	Bracket Placement on Either Side of Glass
36	12	24	=	60	12
42	12	26	=	68	13
48	12	28	=	76	14
54	12	30	=	84	15
60	12	32	=	92	16
66	12	34	=	100	17
72	12	36	=	108	18
78	12	38	=	116	19
84	12	40	=	124	20
90	12	42	=	132	21
96	12	44	=	140	22
102	12	46	=	148	23
108	12	48	=	156	24
114	12	50	=	164	25
120	12	52	=	172	26
126	12	54	=	180	27
132	12	56	=	188	28
138	12	58	=	196	29
144	12	60	=	204	30
150	12	62	=	212	31
156	12	64	=	220	32
162	12	66	=	228	33
168	12	68	=	236	34
174	12	70	=	244	35
180	12	72	=	252	36
186	12	74	=	260	37
192	12	76	=	268	38

*Deduct 7" from a one-way draw.

Hems and Headers. Every drapery, no matter how long, has to have hems and headers. Headers are the "hems" at the top of the drapery They come in various styles, including French- or pinch-pleated, gathered or rod-pocket, box-pleated, cartridge or pipe organ, smocked or shirred, and looped or tab top.

French- or pinch-pleated drapery headers are the most common custom drapery style. Stiff buckram forms a ridged frame that the fabric is sewn around; 4 inches of double fabric is used for commercial drapes and 4 to 6 inches of double fabric is used for custom drapes. Next, the buckram with the fabric sewn in place is three-fold pinch-pleated to the desired fullness. Pin hooks are then positioned in the drapery pleats to hang up on the rod.

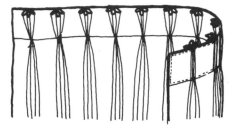
French- or Pinch-Pleated

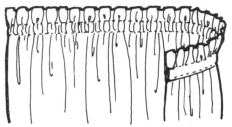
Gathered or Rod Pocket

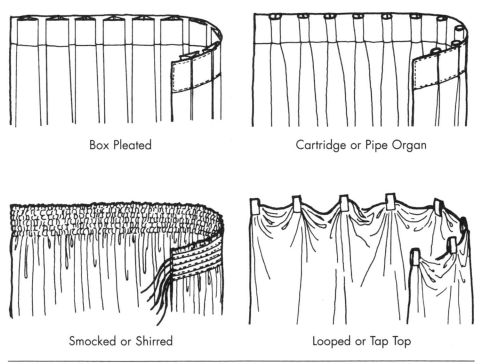

Box Pleated

Cartridge or Pipe Organ

Smocked or Shirred

Looped or Tap Top

Another popular header is the gathered or rod-pocket header. This header has no buckram; instead, it has a fabric rod-pocket casing. A wood pole slips into the rod pocket and the fabric is pushed or gathered along the rod. Often a 1- or 2-inch ruffle is added to the top of the rod pocket.

Box-pleated headers start out the same as the French-pleated headers but are sewn once and pressed flat. The fold of fabric sewn into place creates fullness. Cartridge or pipe-organ pleated headers are made the same way as box pleats except the cartridge pleats are formed differently; instead of pressing the fabric flat, each cartridge is stuffed with rolled crinoline to retain its shape.

Smocked or shirred headers are created by sewing a corded tape to the drapery top. When the four or five woven-in cords are evenly pulled, a smocking effect is created. Smocked headers give draperies made with sheer fabrics up to four times the normal fullness. This treatment can also be used for dust ruffles and vanity skirts.

Looped or tab-top headers are loops of separate fabric sewn onto unpleated, flat drapery made with the drapery fabric, a contrasting fabric, or a braid sewn onto the flat drapery top. A round rod slides through the loops.

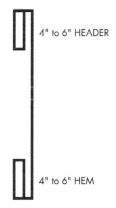

4" to 6" HEADER

4" to 6" HEM

Hems are the finished bottom edges of the drapery They are usually 4 inches of double fabric; however, some draperies have 5 or 6 inches of hems to weigh them down and help them to hang better (all draperies should be corner weighted to keep drapery ends hanging evenly with no flares). Sheer fabrics often are so lightweight that the hem floats and billows. To stabilize these hems and give the fabric weight, sew a bead tape to the hem.

Fullness. The fullness of a drapery is the width of the drapery when it is sewn and pleated together. For example, one 48-inch-wide piece of material will pleat down to a finished width of 16 to 24 inches, depending on how full a drapery is desired. Deep, luxurious folds are more appealing than skimpy ones.

There are three standard fullnesses used for drapery: 2 to 1, 2 1/2 to 1, and 3 to 1. The 2-to-1 fullness is used for bulky, thick fabrics and for less expensive treatments where cost-saving is important. This fullness generally is used to fabricate draperies for apartments, hotels, offices, and other commercial spaces. A fabric width of 48 inches pleated to a finished fullness of 2 to 1 would create a finished drapery 24 inches wide.

Most custom draperies of cottons and blends, lined or unlined, are finished pleated to 2 1/2 to 1. A fabric width of 48 inches pleated to a finished fullness of 2 1/2 to 1 would create a finished drapery 20 inches wide.

Draperies that are pleated to 3-to-1 width are usually sheer, lightweight fabrics. These filmy fabrics need more fullness to keep the finished drapery from looking

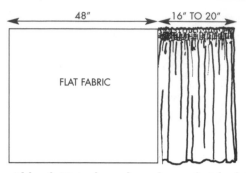

too skimpy. A fabric width of 48 inches pleated to a finished fullness of 3 to 1 would create a finished drapery 16 inches wide.

Any number of widths can be joined together to make draperies properly cover the window area. Fabric off the bolt is typically 48 or 54 inches wide. Drapery lining fabric is generally 48 or 54 inches wide.

Fullness Chart. Use the chart on the right to estimate the fullnesses for commercial, custom, and custom sheer 48- and 54-inch fabrics.

Pattern Matching. Fabrics with pattern repeats play a major role in the design field and are encountered regularly. Cotton prints with various patterns, stripes, and textures are especially popular. There are even solid-colored, textured patterns where a slub thread is repeated at regular intervals. All repeats must be pattern matched before the drapery is fabricated. Finished, pleated drapery hanging at the window with the pattern even slightly off is glaringly noticeable.

A pattern repeat is the lengthwise or crosswise measurement of one design motif to where that exact point is again repeated. There are three types of pattern repeats: straight, half-drop, and random. The straight pattern repeat, which has a repeat ranging from 1 to 36 inches, is the most common. The straight pattern repeat matches up on a straight line horizontally across all widths of fabric.

The repeat height is measured from top to bottom of the motif. The larger the repeat, the more fabric is needed to match the patterns of the different widths.

FULLNESS CHART
(Total Fullness in Inches)

Widths or Panels of Fabric	Commercial 2 to 1		Custom 2½ to 1		Custom Sheers 3 to 1	
	48″	54″	48″	54″	48″	54″
1	23	26	19	21	16	18
1½	35	39	28	32	23	26
2	46	52	37	42	31	35
2½	58	65	46	52	39	44
3	69	78	56	63	46	52
3½	81	91	65	73	54	61
4	92	104	74	84	62	70
4½	104	117	83	94	69	78
5	115	130	92	104	77	87
5½	127	143	102	115	85	96
6	138	156	111	125	92	104
6½	150	169	120	136	100	113
7	161	182	129	146	108	122
7½	173	195	138	156	115	130
8	184	208	148	167	123	139
8½	196	221	157	177	131	148
9	207	234	166	188	138	156
9½	219	247	175	198	146	165
10	230	260	184	208	154	174
10½	242	273	194	219	161	182
11	253	286	203	229	169	191
11½	265	299	212	240	177	200
12	276	312	221	250	184	208
12½	288	325	230	260	192	217
13	299	338	240	271	200	226
13½	311	351	249	281	207	234
14	322	364	258	292	215	243
14½	334	377	267	302	224	252
15	345	390	276	312	230	260
15½	357	403	286	323	238	269
16	368	416	295	333	246	278

The half-drop pattern repeat is the least common pattern; it is more often found in wallpaper patterns. In the half-drop pattern, every other repeated motif appears "dropped" halfway between two other repeats, making the pattern appear to be placed in diagonal lines.

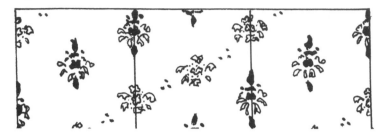

The random pattern repeat is usually used for striped fabrics. A random pattern is a crosswise measurement of a set of stripes encompassing more than one repeat. One repeat would have two stripes in a light tone, another repeat would have one dark repeat and so forth. Striped fabrics with wide repeats may require another whole width of fabric to get the desired finished drapery width.

Split repeats should not appear at either hem and header. Most professional workrooms will place the pattern repeats on the finished treatments in one of two ways. For floor-length treatments, a full repeat will fall just below the heading because the eye travels there first. In shorter-length treatments, such as café style, which hangs from midwindow to window sill, the full repeat will be placed just above the hem for visual balance.

Figuring pattern repeat allowances is done by first figuring the cut length of the drapery. This is the measurement of the total drapery finished length with an allowance of 16 to 20 inches added for hems and headers (the amount of 20 inches will be used in all sample problems as a standard). Twenty inches is the total of the 4-inch double hem and header allowances plus 4 inches for seams and straightening the design. If larger hems are needed, adjust the hem allowance figures accordingly.

Next, divide the cut length by the length of the pattern repeat. This figure gives the number of repeats needed for each cut length. Finally multiply the number of repeats by the length of the repeat to get the total cut length. Therefore, in order to get the total cut length with repeats, you will need three different equations. (This example uses a repeat of 26 inches and a finished length of 96 inches.)

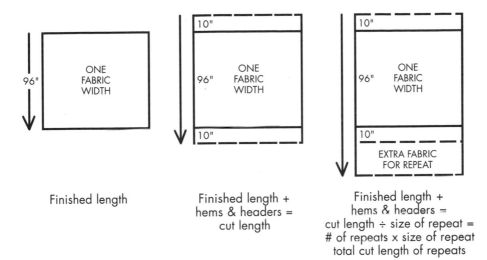

Finished length

Finished length +
hems & headers =
cut length

Finished length +
hems & headers =
cut length ÷ size of repeat =
# of repeats x size of repeat
total cut length of repeats

96" + 20" = 116 cut lengths
116" + 26" = 5 repeats
5 x 26" = 130" total cut length with repeats

Examples

1. Finished length 56", repeat 18".
　　56" + 20" (H.&H.) = 76" cut length
　　76" ÷ 18" (repeat size) = 4.2　5 repeats (always increase fractions)
　　5 x 18" = 90" total cut length with repeats

2. Finished length 84", repeat 12".
　　84" + 20" (H.&H.) = 104" cut length
　　104" ÷ 12" (repeat size) =8.6　9 repeats (always increase fractions)
　　9 x 12" = 108" total cut length with repeats

DRAPERY ESTIMATING

After all the elements and allowances have been explained and diagrammed, put them together for the actual estimate. You will always need two sets of figures for estimating drapery: the finished figures (both width and length) are determined first and then the allowances are added to get the total cut figures.

The starting point in figuring any drapery measurement is determining the finished width and length. The exact width will depend on the type of window and how much of the wall or frame is available to cover with drapery. The length will depend on the design. There are four possible finished drapery lengths: cafe, top of window to apron, top of window to floor, and ceiling to floor.

Certain situations call for extra adjustments in the finished length. Humid climates can affect fabrics, especially open-weave casement styles. When the humidity is high, fabric tends to expand, and when the humidity is low, the same fabric will shrink back to normal. Clients should be informed of this fact so they do not ask you to rehem their draperies every time it rains. The finished length for open weave fabrics in humid climates should be 1 inch off the floor, giving them space to change with the weather.

Another situation requiring adjustment involves contemporary windows that are built without wooden frames and aprons. To keep hems and headers from showing from the outside, the headers should be 5 inches above the window frame and the hems should drop 5 inches below the sill.

Also, when furniture pieces are under a window, the drapery looks best when it ends 1/2 inch short of the furniture, rather than at the sill or apron. This will save in fabric expenses but will also limit the client's option of moving the furniture. In more formal settings, floor-length draperies are more pleasing, even when they are partially covered by furniture.

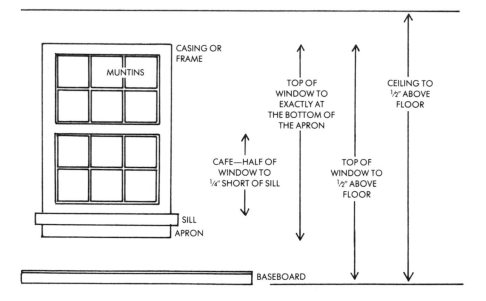

PROBLEM ONE
Estimating Plain or Solid Fabrics Using Fullness Allowances

Basic formula:
Part 1:. Widths. Finished width x fullness + returns & overlaps=total inches wide. Total inches wide divided by fabric width off the bolt=total widths needed to be sewn together.

Part 2: Length. Finished length + hems & headers = cut length.

Part 3: Total. Number of widths x cut length = total length fabric needed in inches.

Total inches divided by 36" (equaling a yard) = total yardage

Example:
The drapery finished width is 106", the finished length is 92" long, custom fullness is 2½ to 1 and the fabric is 54" wide. How much yardage is needed?
Part 1. Width. 106" (finished width) x 2½ (custom fullness) = 12" (returns & over-laps) = 277".

277" (total inches wide) divided by 54" (fabric width) equals 5.1, which equals 5 widths
Part 2. Length. 92" (finished length) + 20" (hems & headers) = 112" cut length.

Part 3. Total. 5 (widths) x 112" (cut length) = 560" total inches.

560" (total inches) divided by 36" (equaling a yard)
equals 15.5 (rounding up) equals 16 yards

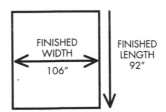

FINISHED WIDTH 106"   FINISHED LENGTH 92"

PROBLEM TWO
Estimating Solid Fabric Using Stacking and Fullness Allowances

When estimating drapery for a window with stacking space, figure the total width first. The stacking amount will add a fourth figure to the equation. Stacking is figured by taking the window opening width and dividing by 3.

Glass width is 84" and stack back of the drapery off the window is desired, the finished length is 92", custom fullness at 2½ to 1 and a solid fabric width is 48". How much yardage is needed?

Part 1 Stacking 84" (glass width) ÷ 3 = 28" (stacking space).

Part 2 Widths 84" (glass width) + 28" (stacking space) =
112" rod and finished drapery width.

112" (finished width) x 2½ (custom fullness)
+ 12" (returns & overlaps) = 292" (total inches)

292" (total inches) ÷ 48" (fabric width) = 6 widths

Part 3 Length 92" (finished length) + 20" (hems & headers) = 112" (cut length).

Part 4 Total 6 (widths) x 112" (cut length) = 672" total length
672" (total inches) ÷ 36" (to convert to yardage)
=18.6 (rounded off) = 19 yards.

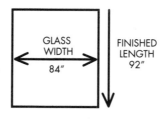

GLASS
WIDTH
84"

FINISHED
LENGTH
92"

PROBLEM THREE
Estimating Pattern Repeated Fabric Using
Stacking and Fullness Allowances

Window widths are always measured and estimated first. To find the correct width of the fabric, start with the stacking space, proceed to estimate fabric widths. Next, the length has to be adjusted to add extra fabric for pattern repeats, and a new length has to be found. Finally, totals are multiplied out to find the total yardage. Glass width is 84", stack back is required; the finished length is 96", custom fullness of 2½ to 1, a pattern repeat of 18" is used and the fabric width is 54". How much yardage is needed?

Part 1 Stacking   84" (glass width) ÷ 3 = 28" (stacking space).

Part 2 Widths   84" (glass width) + 28" (stacking space) = 112" rod and finished drapery width.

112" (finished width) x 2½ (custom fullness) + 12" (returns & overlaps) = 292" (total inches)

292" (total inches) ÷ 54" (fabric width) = 5.4 (rounded up) = 6 widths.

Part 3 Length   96" (finished length) + 20" (hems & headers) = 116" cut length.
Part 4 Repeats 116" (cut length) : 18" (repeat size) = 6.4 (rounded up) = 7 repeats.

Part 5 Length   7 (repeats) x 18" (repeat size) = 126" new cut length.

Part 6 Total   6 (widths) x 126" (new cut length) = 756" (total length). 756" (total length) ÷ 36" (to convert to yardage) = 21 yards

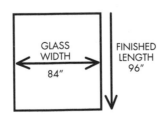

PROBLEM FOUR
Estimating Sheer Fabric Using Stacking and Fullness Allowances

Sheer fabrics, because of their light weight, will always need extra fabric; 3-to-1 fullness is used to make graceful, luxurious sheer draperies. Stacking for sheers is figured exactly the same as in Problem Three.

Glass width is 104", stacking is required, the finished length is 95", sheer fullness of 3 to 1 and the solid fabric width is 54". How much yardage is needed?

Part 1 Stacking   104" (glass width) ÷ 3 = 34.6 (rounded up) = 35" (stacking space).

Part 2 Widths   104" (glass width) + 35" (stacking space) = 139" rod and finished drapery width.

139" (finished width) x 3 (sheer fullness) +12" (returns & overlaps) = 429" (total width inches).

429" (total width inches) ÷ 54" (fabric width) = 7.9 (rounded up) = 8 widths

Part 3 Length   95" (finished length) + 20" (hems & headers) = 115" cut length.

Part 4 Total   8 (widths) x 115" (cut length) = 920" (total inches).

920" (total length) ÷ 36" = 25.5 (rounded up) = 26 yards

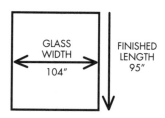

PROBLEM FIVE
Estimating 118" Seamless Fabric Using Stacking and Fullness Allowances

Fabrics manufactured without seams are generally 106 to 118 inches long. The 118-inch length was developed for draperies hanging in interiors with 8-foot ceilings and is more commonly used. This length gives a maximum finished length of 98 inches plus enough fabric for hems and headers. Please note that many seamless fabrics come with hems already put on by the manufacturer.

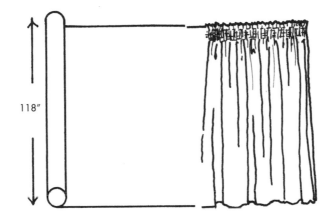

There are many styles of seamless 118-inch draperies, including sheers, embroideries, woven knits, casements, and even some linings. These are domestically manufactured as well as imported from many European countries. Seamless draperies offer many advantages, including no visible vertical seams in finished hanging draperies, no puckered seams, and no shrinking or sagging. These draperies hang more smoothly because they were woven as one long fabric rather than as shorter fabrics needing to be sewn together. There is no pattern matching with seamless fabrics; the pattern is already woven into the fabric. Seamless fabrics look like they cost more, but in reality one yard of 118-inch-long fabric has nearly two and a half times more material than 45- or 48-inch-long fabrics. (Always use custom fullness of 2 1/2 to 1 or sheer fullness of 3 to 1 in calculating yardage to keep these sheer fabric from looking skimpy.)

Seamless 118-inch drapery fabric has the easiest yardage to calculate because you do not need to figure the length. However, the finished length does need to be specified on the work order.

Glass width 108", stacking is required, the finished length is 98", sheer fullness of 3 to 1 and the fabric is 118". How much fabric is needed?

Part 1 Stacking 108" (glass width) ÷ 3 = 36" (stacking space).

Part 2 Widths 108" (glass width) + 36" (stacking space) = 144" rod and finished drapery width.

144" (finished width) x 3 (sheer fullness) + 12" (returns & overlaps) = 444" (total inches)

No widths are needed with 118" fabrics

Part 3 Length 98" (finished length) + 20" (hems & headers) = 118" (cut length).

Part 4 total 444" (total inches) ÷ 36" (to convert to yardage) = 12.3 (rounded up) = 13 yards.

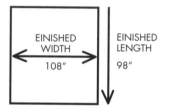

COST ESTIMATING

When estimating costs for a total drapery treatment, there will be two labor costs: one from the drapery workroom and one from the installer. Those actual costs can be calculated from their current price sheets. There will also be two material costs: one for the fabrics and one for the rods and hardware. These costs will always be changing as inflation pushes the prices upward and as new products are introduced. Fabric prices are based on a per-yard cost and rods are based on a per-foot cost.

TIME ESTIMATING

Time must be estimated for both fabrication and installation. Certain variables will affect each.

Fabrication. Custom draperies can take anywhere from three to six weeks to fabricate. There are many people involved in this process and problems can occur anywhere along the way. One of the busiest times of the year for any drapery workroom is right before the Christmas holidays. As a general rule, most workrooms will not take any new orders from Thanksgiving through to the new year. This situation should be kept in mind as clients rush to order new draperies before Christmas.

The fabrication process starts when you fill out the work order and deliver it with a 50 percent deposit in person or by mail to the workroom, keeping a copy for reference in case the workroom has any questions. This can take from one to about four days.

Next, the fabric is ordered. Most fabric companies will take phone orders and immediately qualify the yardage as "in stock" or "back-ordered." The fabric company will either ship the order to you or directly to the workroom with the proper side mark (name of client or job). Shipping can take from two to six days depending on how far away the fabric company is located. Fabric companies will also ship next-day air and overnight on rush orders for an added charge.

Drapery workrooms will record on the work order the date of the order, the date all fabrics were received for the job, and the promised delivery date. It is a good idea to check periodically with the workroom to make sure fabrics have arrived and are not flawed.

After the workroom has received all fabrics, the order goes into fabrication. Since custom draperies are so specialized, an entire drapery order could take three to four weeks to fabricate. This depends on the amount of draperies, the kinds of fabrics (casements take longer to hem, for example), the intricacy of the coordinating components, such as cornices, and the work involved. The workroom will give you an estimated finish date before beginning the job.

Installation. When the fabrication of the draperies is almost finished, you must notify the installer so that he or she can schedule the installation. The installer has to pick up the proper rods and other hardware so that he or she can precut or shape any rods and set up the equipment for the installation. From the beginning of the order to the installation it usually takes three to six weeks. Before setting up actual installation dates, contact the client to confirm that the dates are acceptable to him or her.

On the day of installation, the designer needs to be at the job site. Many times the installer will need extra direction and/or the client needs to be distracted so the installer can complete his or her work. If there are any problems, the designer, client, and installer can review options for a satisfactory solution.

SELECTING A DRAPERY WORKROOM

Much of residential interior design and some of commercial design work encompasses drapery treatments. Drapery design and fabrication can be one of the most important elements in a design project, which makes selecting a drapery workroom critical to the success of each project.

When looking for a drapery workroom, check in local business directories and ask other designers for recommendations. Many people suggest using drapery workrooms that have been in business for at least ten years. When you call a workroom, ask for references, especially other designers they work for, and call these references, adding their comments to your subcontractor files.

You should try to personally inspect a prospective drapery workroom and look at their work-in-progress plus their finished draperies. Ask for a price sheet and read it over, asking any questions before leaving. Every workroom has quality standards and they can be seen by reading through their price sheet. Some of those standards should include double hems and headers, 1 1/2-inch double side seams, blind stitched bottom and side hems, all seams serged and overlocked, all draperies corner weighted, and pleating custom tacked with extra thread. Pleating multiple-width draperies to hide seams and pattern matching are also standards. The draperies also need to be fan folded before they leave the workroom so that when they are hung the fold will hang straight down from the pleat at the header.

Since every drapery design project is unique and customized to the client's needs, you need a workroom that has the ability to be creative but will also pay attention to detail. Quite often it is the detail work that will separate an average workroom from one that does top-quality work. Details include pattern-matching stripes; hemming on the job for those sagging, uneven floors; slightly overlapping seams for banding so shadows do not occur; and all kinds of intricate work. For example, casement fabrics always stretch, so the better workrooms hang casement draperies a week before hemming. The better workrooms also candle all fabrics before they are cut, and many have candling tables. Candling requires the fabric to be passed over a light source so that flaws can be seen before the draperies are fabricated and hung at a window Drapery workroom services should include supplying a qualified installer, remeasuring for any job, and building and installing cornices, lambrequins, and cantonnieres. However, installation is not always provided by a workroom. There are some independent installers who will work with several workrooms and/or designers.

In addition, some drapery workrooms have the machinery and skilled workers to provide both drapery and bedcovering products for the designer. It is more convenient to use a workroom that provides both services; if you use two separate workrooms, then fabrics have to be ordered together and sent to two different locations.

After you find the perfect workroom, try to build a sound relationship. The practice of using a work-order form and having it signed by the workroom is a good way to avoid misunderstandings. A workroom can become a valuable part of your design team.

EXAMPLE OF FINAL DRAPERY COSTS

Mr. and Mrs. Bennett hired an interior designer to design unique and customized drapery treatments for their master bedroom. They chose a lace sheer underdrapery, lined cotton printed traverse draperies, and a balloon valance with a box-pleated header. They wanted all the draperies to stack off the window because of their wonderful garden view.

The lace sheer selected was 54 inches wide. The printed cotton had a 24-inch repeat and was 54 inches wide. The lining fabric was also 54 inches wide.

Window Measurements.

Glass width is 96", stack back of the drapery is required, the finished length is 97", sheer fullness 3 to 1 and the solid fabric width is 54" wide.

Sheer Fabric (using sheer drapery formula on page 106)

Part 1 Stacking   96" (glass width) ÷ 3 = 32" (stacking space).

Part 2 Widths   96" (glass width) + 32" (stacking space) = 128" rod and finished drapery width.

128" (finished width) x 3 (sheer fullness) + 12" (returns & overlaps) = 396" (total width)

396" (total width) ÷ 54" (fabric width) = 7.3 (rounded up) = 8 widths

Part 3 Length   97" (finished length) + 20" (hems & headers) = 117" cut length.

Part 4 Total   8 (widths) x 117" (cut length) = 936" (total inches).

936" (total inches) ÷ 36" (to convert to yardage) = 26 yards

Cotton Print (Using repeat formula on page 105)

The other change in this example concerns the cotton print return. Returns are usually 3 to 3½ inches deep. Each time another rod and layer of drapery is added to a treatment, a longer return is needed to get past the first rod and drapery. This cotton print needs to return to the wall past the sheers which will add another 6" to the return resulting in an 18" return instead of the normal 12" return (see page 92).

Part 1 Stacking   96" (glass width) ÷ 3 = 32" (stacking space).

Part 2 Widths   96" (glass width) + 32" (stacking space) = 128" rod and finished drapery width.

128" (finished width) x 2½ (custom fullness) + 18" (returns & overlaps) = 338" (total width)

338" (total width) ÷ 54" (fabric width) = 6.2 (rounded up) = 7 widths

Part 3 Length   97" (finished length) + 20" (hems & headers) =
117" cut length.

Part 4 Repeats   117" (cut length) ÷ 24" (repeat size) =
4.8 (rounded up) = 5 repeats.

Part 5 Length   5 (repeats) x 24" (repeat size) = 120" (new cut length)

Part 6 Total   7 (widths) x 120" (new cut length) = 840" (total length)

840" (total length) ÷ 36" (to convert to yardage) =
23.3 (rounded up) = 24 yards

Lining
You'll need the same amount of lining as the cotton print fabric.

Valance (using formula on page 103)
The valance has to have side returns over both the sheer drapery and the cotton print drapery, which means the returns are going to be 6 inches longer on each side to reach the wall. The new return is 24" (see page 92). Also, the valance is out of a solid colored fabric (no repeats). The finished length for the valance is 18".

Part 1 Stacking   96" (glass width) ÷ 3 = 32" (stacking space).

Part 2 Widths   96" (glass width) + 32" (stacking space) =
128" finished valance width.

128" (finished width) x 2½ (custom fullness)
+ 24" (returns & overlaps) = 344" (total width)
344" (total width) ÷ 54" (fabric width) =
6.3 (rounded up) = 7 widths

Part 3 Length   18" (finished length) + 20" (hems & headers) = 38" Cut length.

Part 4 Total   7 (widths) x 38" (cut length) = 266" (total inches).
266" (total inches) ÷ 36" (to convert to yardage) =
7.3 (rounded up) = 8 yards

FINAL ESTIMATE

Sheers:

Fabric: Pattern–Lacey; color–Ivory; 26 yards @ $21.00 * =	$546.00
Labor: 8 Widths @ $20.00 =	160.00

Cotton Print:

Pattern–Flora; color–Spring; 24 yards @ $43.00 =	1,032.00
Labor: 7 Widths @ $20.00 =	140.00

Lining:

Pattern–Sateena; color–Ivory; 24 yards @ $ 7.10 =	170.40
Labor: 7 widths @ $4.00 =	28.00

Valance:

Pattern–Saigon; color–Sage; 8 yards @ $33.00 =	264.00
Labor: 7 widths (balloon style) @ $15.00 =	105.00

Rods:

Heavy-duty, double traverse rod & hardware for lined cotton print & sheer drapery; 10.6 foot @ $15.00 =	159.90

Valance Rod:

Balloon valance rod & hardware 11 foot @ $10.00 =	110.00

Installation Labor:

Each rod per foot; 3 rods x 33 feet @ $10.00 =	330.00

	Subtotal	$3,044.90
	Tax 7.5% **	203.61
	TOTAL	$3,248.51

Estimated time to fabricate: 2 to 4 weeks, after receipt of all fabrics.

* All figures based on 2001 Phoenix, Arizona prices.

** Each state would calculate tax differently according to their state laws. Some states apply tax on newly manufactured products only. Draperies are considered a new product, therefore this labor is taxed. Check your state laws to see what sale and use taxes apply.

Drapery Work Order

Date: March 19, 2001

P.O. # 1050

Designer: Carol Sumpter

Address: 7605 Scottsdale Road
Scottsdale AZ

Phone: (480) 956-5656

Address: Mr. & Mrs. J. Bennett
4300 Gainey Ranch
Scottsdale, AZ

Phone: (480) 975-5777

Date Fabric Received: March 19, 2001

Date Promised: April 9, 2001

Workroom: Evelyn's Drapery

Address: 1234 White Road
Scottsdale AZ

Phone: (480) 989-5500

	Room	Qty.	Pair	Panel L or R	Fabric Co.	Pattern	Color	Repeat	No. Widths	Rod Size	Returns	Finished Width	Finished Length	Total Yards	Lined	Rod Type	H & H Size
1. Drapes	L	1	yes	0	P.+P.	Flora	Multi	24"	7	128"	6"	128"	96"	24	yes	Traverse	90"
2. Sheer	L	1	yes	0	P.+P.	Lacey	Ivory	0	8	128"	3"	128"	96"	26	No	Traverse	90"
3. Valance	L	1	yes	Balloon Val.	P.+P.	Saigon	Sage	0	7	140"	12"	140"	18"	9	No	Vali. Rod	0
4.																	
5.																	
6.																	
7.																	
8.																	

Drapery

Drapery Work Order

Date: _____

P.O. # _____

Designer: _____

Address: _____

Phone: _____

Address: _____

Phone: _____

Date Fabric Received: _____

Date Promised: _____

Workroom: _____

Address: _____

Phone: _____

Drapery																
Room	Qty.	Pair	Panel L or R	Fabric Co.	Pattern	Color	Repeat	No. Widths	Rod Size	Returns	Finished Width	Finished Length	Total Yards	Lined	Rod Type	H & H Size
1.																
2.																
3.																
4.																
5.																
6.																
7.																
8.																

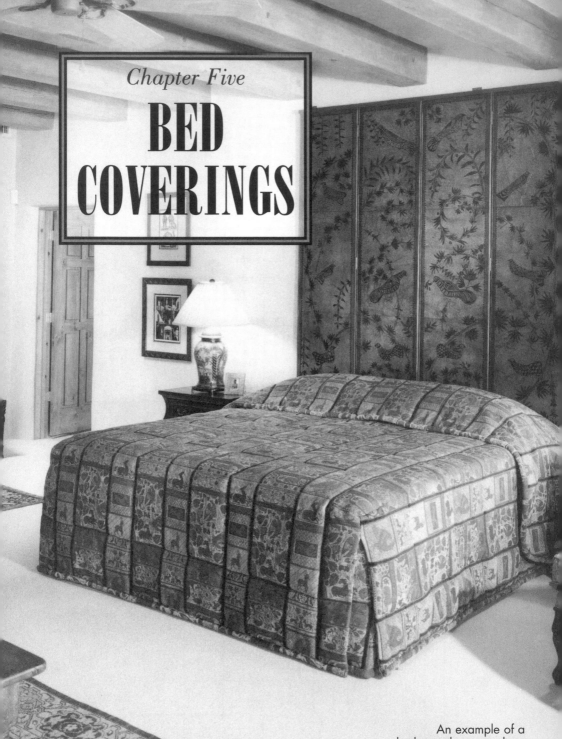

Chapter Five

BED COVERINGS

An example of a bedspread reverse sham and two fitted corners with tongues or gussets.

S ince Egyptian times, bed coverings have been elaborate and elegant, with styles over the years including canopies, valances, draperies, dust ruffles, comforters, pillows, shams, and multiple spreads. Egyptian beds of royalty were upholstered in cotton or painted leathers and sometimes covered with fabrics in gold or silver. The bed legs were wood carved with decorative animal designs terminating in paw feet. Bed covers consisted of layers of linen sheets that were cool during hot desert nights.

The Egyptians also came up with one of the first known bed pillows: a rectangular block with a round pedestal supporting a curved headrest.

In about the same period, the Greeks also developed a bed with carved legs. Their animal designs on these legs were more stylized and graceful than those of the Egyptians. The Greeks also utilized disk-turned leg designs that were just as popular as the animal forms.

Grecian bed frames were made of wood, with carvings and trimmings accented in beautiful patterns of ivory, metal, and stone inlays. The mattress portion had an upholstered chaise design with a softly reclining headrest. Extra soft cushion-style pillows were used for comfort. The Greeks also used another style of bed that utilized a form of springs-a platform was made out of strips of leather criss-crossed over a frame, and animal skins were spread over this support.

The Roman beds of this period, like much of Roman design, were copied and adapted from Grecian forms and design principles. The Romans also had raised upholstered beds with disk-turned or carved-wood animal legs. However, the Romans' trimmings were even more elaborate than those of either the Egyptians or the Greeks, using gold, bronze, and silver inlays.

The Pompeians (69 A. D.) constructed their bed frames from wood and/or metal. They then stretched supporting straps of thin metal or braided ropes on the bed frames from headboard to footboard, and placed a plump mattress filled with straw, feathers, and/or wool on top of the straps. They covered the mattress with elaborate and costly oriental woven textiles and silk cushions. For comfort in the mild climate, they used lightweight top covers.

In the colder climates, warmth was and continues to be the primary purpose for bed coverings. In the ancient past animal furs and hides were used. The easiest to obtain and most comfortable to use were deer, bear, buffalo, and other furs.

Before and during the Middles Ages, beds were piles of leaves on the floor covered with skins. In time, this design progressed into shallow boxes or chests filled with leaves and moss. It was not until the early Middle Ages (500–700) that mattresses filled with feathers, wool, and hair were used. As time passed, the beds themselves were raised off the ground and supported by legs.

Drafty and damp castles, manor houses, and villas of the eleventh century made enclosed heavily draped beds popular. It was much warmer under a down comforter if heavy velvet or tapestry hung closed around the bed to keep out the northern chill. Privacy was another factor for using bed drapery. Regardless of social

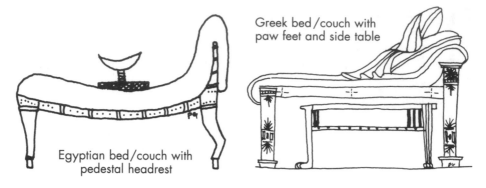

Greek bed/couch with paw feet and side table

Egyptian bed/couch with pedestal headrest

Pompeii bronze bed with disk-turned legs

Seventeenth-century state bed from Rushbrooke Hall, England (1685). Bed hangings were pulled closed for warmth and privacy.

A massive Elizabethan bed from the sixteenth century.

Empress Josephine's bedchamber (1790). The walls were draped in red silk and the bed draperies were lined with ermine. This royal chamber combines touches of Egypt. Greece, and Rome.

American Victorian brass bed

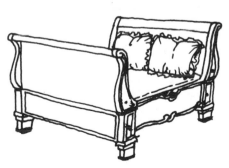

French sleigh bed

American four-poster bed with canopy and drapery

status, the living room during the day was often the bedroom at night. A separate sleeping room was virtually unknown until the eighteenth century.

The French attached enormous importance to the bed as a symbol of wealth and status. Louis XIII, Louis XIV, Louis XV, and Louis XVI (1610–1790) each held court in his bed, and elaborate ceremony was attached to their daily activities of getting up and getting dressed in front of a few privileged guests. In fact, the king's bed was held in higher regard than his throne. All aristocrats who could afford to do so lavished great amounts of money to emulate this grandeur. The state bed was often composed of over 30 textile parts using yards of embroidery and fringes— costing vast fortunes.

In England, during Queen Elizabeth I's reign, the state bed had reached its zenith of exaggeration and expense. The bed remained an immense symbol of wealth and social position up through the reign of Queen Anne.

By the time of the Industrial Revolution (1839), both beds and rooms had been scaled down. Beds and their coverings had become simpler and far less expensive. The woodworking and drapery were vastly toned down—although elaborate styles continued to appear (for example, the angel bed with suspended canopy and curtains looped back, the sleek sleigh bed, and the four-poster bed style emerged at this time in Europe).

Today many beds can be covered simply or elaborately in both historical or contemporary styles. The design of any bedroom will be dominated by the bed or beds in that room, strongly affecting the room's character with colors, patterns, and style, expressing the occupant's outlook and personality

BED COVERING BASICS

In order to measure and estimate for bed coverings, it is important to have an understanding of the different materials and styles available.

Bed covering materials. The materials used for bed coverings are the same fabrics as those used for draperies, which include silks, linens, cottons, rayon, nylon, polyester, acetate, and blends. They come in a vast selection of patterns, fiber content, styles, prices, and quality. Often, designer sheets are used to make comforters, bedspreads, shams, dusters, and decorative pillows. Fabrics used for drapery and bed coverings come in widths of 36, 48, 54 inches, although 36 and 48 inch fabrics are rarely used anymore. Many workrooms will not work with them; if they do, they may charge more for the extra work require.

Bedspreads. Today, bed coverings are again elegant and often elaborate, using many layers of treatments and stacks of decorative pillows. The bedspread is primarily an ornamental cover which reaches to the floor, but it is also used by some as part of the sleeping covers, especially in cold climates. Some of the more popular styles are the throw, the throw with jumbo welt, the throw with scalloped edge,

Bedspread Styles and Forms

Throw Style

Throw Style with Jumbo
Welt 1", 2" or 3"

Throw Style with
Scalloped Edge

2 Fitted Corners with
Tongues or Gussets

4 Fitted Corners with
Tongues or Gussets

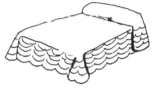

Throw Style with
Scalloped Rows

Plain or Quilted Top
with Shirred Drop

Plain or Quilted Top with
Double-Shirred Drop

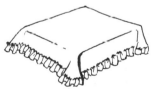

Throw Style with
Ruffled Bottom Edge

Fitted Waterfall

Contoured & Fitted

Any Bedspread Style
with Reverse Sham

fitted corners with tongues and gussets, fitted corners with a top welt, shirred drops, fitted waterfall, contoured and fitted, and reverse sham.

Throw Style. A throw bedspread is the easiest and least expensive spread to make or have made. One fabric is used with or without a filling or a lining. The throw is hemmed on all sides, has rounded foot corners, has a 21" drop, and uses a pillow tuck—fabric tucked under the pillow and folded back over the pillow—to hide the pillows. Estimating a custom throw bedspread is done by first measuring the bed and then dividing the fabric width into the total cuts. (See example on page 134.)

Throw with Jumbo Welt. The jumbo welt is a thick cotton cord that can be 1, 2, or 3 inches or more in thickness. Jumbo welts add weight to the spread and make its corners flare out considerably at the foot. Jumbo welts are a wonderful accent in a contrasting fabric or color. Additional textural effects can be achieved by gathering the fabric on the jumbo welt.

When estimating for a jumbo welt, measure the length around three sides of the bed and add another half of that total to get enough fabric for the flare at the foot of the bed. For example, a 60" x 80" queen-size bed will measure 220 inches around for the two sides and the foot. Add 110 inches more for the two flares at the foot and the total amount of welt cord needed will be 330 inches or 9 linear (straight or running) yards.

Throw with a Scalloped Edge. Scalloped edges, which are semicircle curves, may be wide (12 to 18 inches) or narrow (6 inches or less). The narrower size gives a more traditional look while the wider scallop can be more contemporary in design. Be sure to indicate on your work order what size you require. Scallops can also be made in rows; however, check with your workroom to make sure they will do this work. A custom scalloped-edge throw bedspread will take longer to make, so the labor costs will be higher. The yardage required for a scalloped edge throw is the same as for a regular throw-style bedspread.

Fitted Corners with Tongues or Gussets. Both terms are correct and they both provide a fitted corner. Split corners with a fabric insert give a more tailored appearance. Functionally fitted corners work best on a four-poster bed, a day bed, or a trundle bed. The spread will fit around the legs of the bed more easily. Estimated yardage is the same as for a throw-style bedspread and there is no extra labor charge.

Shirred Drops. The shirred drop, usually 20 to 21 inches, starts at the top edge of the bedspread and drops to the floor in gathered ruffles. This very graceful design is usually used for lighter weight fabrics, especially sheers, laces, and silks. You can also use a double-shirred design, but make sure the workroom can do it. To estimate yardage, find out how many fabric widths will fit the top by measuring the center piece of fabric and any split, then measure drops as if they were dusters.

Next, measure the three sides of the bed and double it to get fullness of the gathering of the sides.

Fitted Waterfall. The fitted waterfall has both sides fitted and the end drop draped over so that it smoothly wraps or falls over the end of the bed. This is a very smooth, tailored look that, coupled with a quilting, makes an unusual bedspread. Estimating yardage is the same as for a throw-style bedspread. The workroom tailors the end and sides.

Contoured and Fitted. The contoured-and-fitted bedspread closely fits the shape of the mattress, with corners sewn down like a sheet to the top of the bed. Usually the box springs are upholstered in the same fabric. This style requires careful measurements to get an upholstered look and the combined efforts of an upholsterer and the bedspread workroom. The fitted bedspread is both measured and estimated using the same methods as for the throw-style bedspread with a shorter 14-inch drop instead of a 21-inch drop. The upholstered platform is measured and estimated using straight fabric widths.

Any Bedspread Style with Reverse Sham. A reverse sham is a piece of fabric sewn at the top of the bedspread so that it folds over the top of the pillow. The reverse sham can be used on any bedspread style. Estimating for a reverse sham is done by referring to the chart. For example, according to the chart on page 140, a standard 20 x 30 twin pillow sham would require two yards of 48-inch fabric.

Coverlets, Comforters and Duvets. Coverlets, comforters, and duvets are bed coverings that only cover the mattress and do not reach the floor. The current popularity of the duvet or coverlet meets the practical needs of a light weight bed cover that is easier to manage than a bedspread when making the bed in the morning. They are also used for warmth, and can be less expensive and decorative than bedspreads.

Coverlets. Coverlets look most like bedspreads except they only have a 12 to 16 inch drop, depending on the height of the bed. Some four poster beds can require a longer drop than usual. Coverlets are single thicknesses of fabric, plain or quilted, used for four-poster beds, antique beds, brass beds, day beds and normal beds usually in combination with a dust ruffle or bed skirt.

Comforters. Comforters are usually quilted with a layer of light, bulky filling sewn between two layers of fabric so that warmth is trapped. They should be 18 inches wider than your bed, usually with a 12 to 14 inch drop, no pillow tuck, and square or round corners. They can be filled with synthetic polyester of 4, 8, 12, or 16 ounces, or silk, goose down or a mixture of down and feathers. For reversible comforters, order twice as much fabric to cover both sides.

Duvets and Covers. Duvets are bed coverings constructed with a layer of light, bulky filling—usually down and feathers—sewn between two layers of fabric. Duvets have a removable cover for cleaning. The construction is wall channeled— an inner wall of fabric separates the channels so the down will not shift or bunch up. These bed coverings have long been used in cold European countries because you can sleep comfortably under them in either sub-zero or 75-degree weather. A duvet will maintain the body's temperature without the weight of a blanket. (There are natural duvet fillings for those who are allergic to feathers, which are made from wool, wool cashmere, cotton, or silks.)

Duvet covers are usually made from two fabrics sewn together on three sides. The fourth side has a zipper, snaps, or buttons so that the duvet can be removed and the cover washed.

Dusters. A duster is a skirt that hangs from a box spring to the floor. Dusters are sewn to a plain white cotton sheeting that is laid flat between the mattress and the box springs.

Fabric tape with snaps or Velcro can also be sewn to both the sheeting and duster or directly to the box spring for ease in washing the duster. This technique saves time and energy by enabling the duster to be pulled off from the sheeting, which stays between the mattress and box springs. It also saves the sheeting and duster from tearing on electric beds where the bed position is constantly being moved. The Velcro-attached duster is the best way to fit a trundle bed as well. Three separate pieces of dust ruffle can easily be adjusted and overlapped at the corners when Velcro is used (some workrooms will construct a duster this way for an extra charge). All dusters must be measured separately due to the various lengths and widths of beds by measuring the width and drop (see figure on page 130).

The more popular styles of dusters are fitted or tailored, shirred or gathered, and box-pleated.

Fitted or tailored. A fitted or tailored custom duster is a straight, smooth piece of fabric that hangs from the box springs to the floor. The drop measurement is usually 12 to 14 inches plus 4 inches for seams. One pleat is generally made per side in the center and one at each corner at the foot of the bed, which takes 36 inches. To estimate yardage, measure three sides of the bed, add 36 inches for pleats and divide by the fabric width. Then multiply by the drop measurement and divide by 36 to get total yardage. For example: A queen-size bed is 60 inches x 80 inches and the total length around the sides and foot is 220 inches. Add 36 inches for pleats to get a total of 256 inches, which divided by 54-inch fabric equals 5 widths. The drop is 14 inches multiplied by 5 widths equals 70 inches, divided by 36 equals 2 yards. It is always better to round up.

Shirred or gathered. A shirred or gathered custom duster is a gathered piece of fabric that hangs from the box springs to the floor. The drop measurement is usually 12 to 14 inches plus 4 inches for seams. To estimate for a gathered duster, follow

Coverlets, Comforters & Duvets

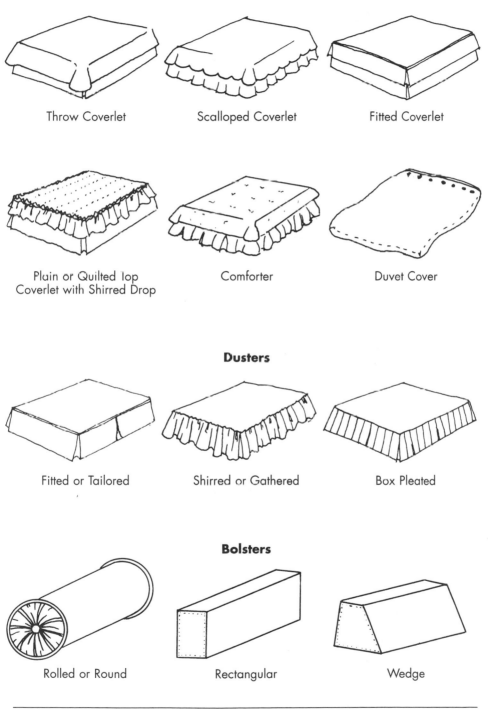

Throw Coverlet   Scalloped Coverlet   Fitted Coverlet

Plain or Quilted Top
Coverlet with Shirred Drop   Comforter   Duvet Cover

Dusters

Fitted or Tailored   Shirred or Gathered   Box Pleated

Bolsters

Rolled or Round   Rectangular   Wedge

Pillow Shams

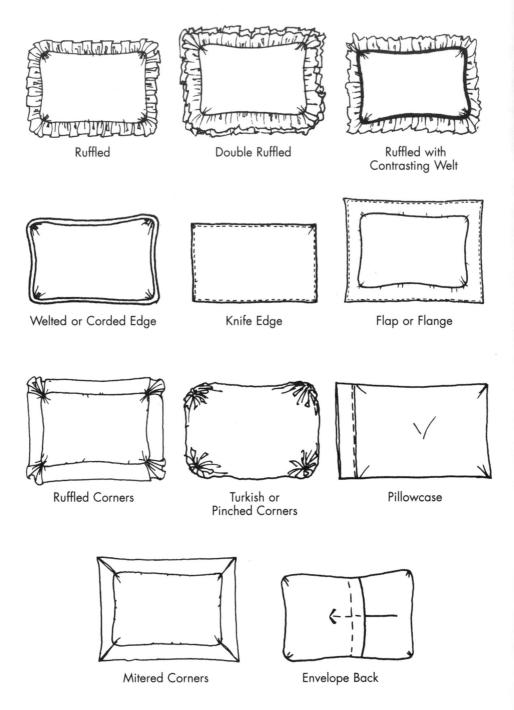

Ruffled

Double Ruffled

Ruffled with
Contrasting Welt

Welted or Corded Edge

Knife Edge

Flap or Flange

Ruffled Corners

Turkish or
Pinched Corners

Pillowcase

Mitered Corners

Envelope Back

the same procedure as that for gathered dusters and multiply the final yardage by 2 to get double fullness. All shirred or pleated dusters are 2 to 3 times fullness.

Box-pleated. The box-pleated duster is usually made with 4-inch pleats; however, smaller or larger pleat sizes can be specified. This duster hangs from the box springs to the floor with a drop of 12 to 14 inches plus 4 inches for seams. To estimate yardage, follow the same directions as for a fitted duster and multiply the final yardage by 2½. Because of the inside pleats, a box-pleated duster uses extra fabric. However, a beautiful effect is created when the inside pleat is a contrasting color to the outside pleat. To estimate this treatment, just split the yardage for equal amounts of colored fabric.

Bolsters. Bolsters are longer, firmer pillows 36 to 42 inches long used on day beds or trundle beds. They are made in three standard styles: round, rectangular, and wedge. Bolsters are most commonly used on day beds instead of pillows or in combination with pillows. Bolsters can vary in size as well as styles. Rectangular and wedge bolsters generally are 36 inches wide and act as back rests for day beds or trundle beds. Because of its angled shape, the wedge bolster is the most common bolster style. Most often, bolsters are quilted or zippered. Round or rolled bolsters can have a sunburst, pleated, gathered or a plain design on the ends.

Pillow Shams. Pillow shams are pillow covers that help keep the pillows clean while adding a decorative element. They can be made from the same fabric as the bed coverings, a contrasting fabric, or a combination of both.

Custom pillow shams can be creative decorator bed accents embellished with lace overlays, fringes, braids, tassels, buttons and bows. Ruffled pillow shams offer added contrast to bed coverings; they can be made in different fabrics or colors from the body of the sham. An even more elaborate treatment is to have double rows of contrasting ruffles with welts and cords in solid or striped fabric sewn between the ruffles and body of the sham.

Sham edges come in various styles: the knife edge—a plain, unadorned edging; the flanged edge—a flat piece of fabric about 2½ to 4 inches wide sewn to the outside edge of the sham body (this can be of contrasting pattern or color for added accent, or banded); and the mitered edge—a flanged edge with mitered corners. Flanged pillow edges can be filled with batting to make them stand up instead of flopping over. An added welt can give a softer appearance to an otherwise squared—off pillow edge.

Ruffled corners can dress up a plain sham edge. One style is Turkish corners (also known as pinched or butterfly), in which each square corner is gathered in place on the inside of the pillow, giving the outside corner a pinched look. Another style, the pillow-case sham, is literally the same style and design as a pillowcase. The designer may want to use the same fabric as the bedspread and tie it with a draw-string at one end. The envelope-back sham—one flap folded under the other—is designed to have a finished look and is easily removed for cleaning.

Quilting. Quilting for bedspreads, comforters, coverlets, shams, and bolster covers is done one of two ways: standard or hand-guided. There are many basic or standard patterns of quilting available from workrooms at no extra charge. In standard quilting, the quilting machine does all the work of pushing and quilting the

Standard Quilting Patterns

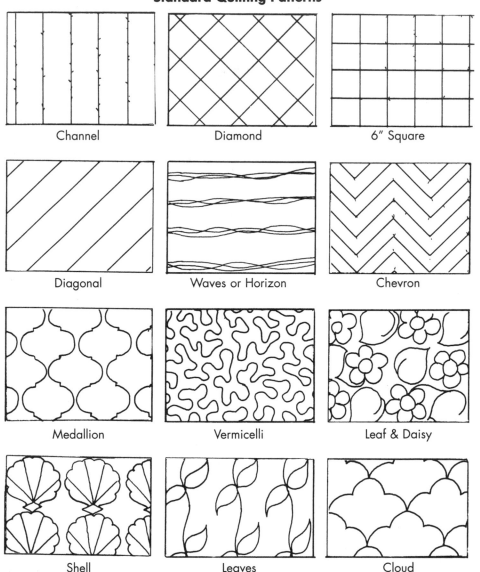

Channel	Diamond	6" Square
Diagonal	Waves or Horizon	Chevron
Medallion	Vermicelli	Leaf & Daisy
Shell	Leaves	Cloud

fabric. Some standard quilting patterns are chevron, medallion, vermicelli, shells, leaves, and clouds. Most surprising is the extra expense charged to quilt square, diamond, channel, and diagonal patterns. These patterns are expensive to quilt because someone has to hand-draw the pattern onto the fabric with chalk to keep the lines straight. Hand-guided quilting patterns or outlines are most expensive because someone has to stand over the machine and guide the needle around the flowers, leaves, and accents on the fabric pattern.

Most quilting companies will use a monofilament thread because it is cheaper than cotton. However, mercerized cotton thread, which has been treated with a chemical to give it added strength and luster, is preferable. Better workrooms will use two spools of cotton thread in two of the predominant colors in the fabric for a truly custom-quilted look.

Polyester fiberfill is the industry standard for filling. It can be specified in 4-, 6-, 8-, 10-, 12-, and 16-ounce weights, with 6- and 8-ounce the average used. The higher the number of ounces, the heavier the finished bedspread or comforter will be. Many people do not care for heavy bed coverings, so be sure to discuss the weight of the polyfill with the client before ordering.

Unless you order or specify another fabric for the backing, the workroom will use a high-count cotton/polyester in white. You will always need a 10 percent fabric allowance for the quilting process, so be sure to order another half-yard or so. In addition, the thicker the filling, the more yardage will be taken up by the quilting process: up to 15 percent extra yardage, depending on the filling.

HOW TO MEASURE FOR BED COVERS

All beds must be individually measured. Although most bed sizes are standardized, the way beds are used can affect their measurements. One client might use many covers, requiring more material for the bedspread to lay properly Another may use a bed cushion of a foam, egg-crate pad that will easily add 1½ to 2 inches or more to the bedspread drop. A third client may have a customized platform under the box springs instead of a metal bed frame. There are as many different bed measurements as there are clients.

Today's Typical Bed:

MATTRESS CAP

BOX SPRINGS

BED FRAME

CASTERS

Proper Measurements

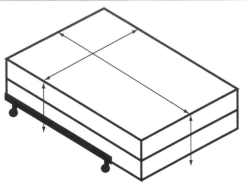

1. Length   Head to foot to floor
2. Width   Side to side
3. Drop   Top of bed to floor
   or bottom of mattress

Basic Rules for Bed covers

Always: Measure the bed with all bed linens and blankets on.

Measure the bed from head to foot.

Measure the drop from the top of the bed to the floor on any side.

Include an allowance of 10 percent of fabric when quilting.

Put seams on the sides; never put a seam down the center of the bedspread.

Wrong

SEAM

48"or 54"
WIDE
FABRIC

No seam down center

Right

SEAM   SEAM

Center of bed

Standard Bed Sizes				
	Width		Length	Drops
Twin	39	×	75 (80 long)	21"—26"
Full	54	×	75	21"—26"
Queen	60	×	80	21"—26"
King	72	×	80	21"—26"
California King	72	×	84	21"—26"
Eastern King	76	×	80	21"—26"
*Dual King (regular twin)	78	×	75	21"—26"
*Dual King (long twin)	78	×	80	21"—26"

* Dual king beds are two twin size beds pushed together and covered with one bedspread. They come in two or more lengths, depending on the size of the twin bed.

Standard Pillow Sizes (for Shams)		Standard Custom Throw Pillows
Twin	20″ × 26″	12″ × 12″
Full	20″ × 26″	16″ × 16″
Queen	20″ × 26″	20″ × 20″
King	20″ × 26″	30″ × 30″

Measuring for Dusters, Bolsters, and Pillows. Measuring for dusters, bolsters, and pillows is done either by measuring existing items or by using the standard charts. For a duster, measure all three sides of the bed plus the drop with a metal tape measure. For a plain, straight duster, figure the width around the sides and foot of the bed. If the duster is gathered, double the total length around the bed for desired fullness. Most bolsters are 36 to 42 inches wide, which nicely fits one width of 48- or 54-inch fabric. Measure around the bolster for the length of fabric needed and add another 10 percent if the fabric is quilted.

Pillows are easy to estimate. One yard of 54-inch fabric could easily fit two to three small 14 x 14-inch pillows depending on the design requirements. If the pillow is 24 x 24 inches, only one yard of 54-inch fabric is required; an extra 1/2 yard is needed to add a ruffle.

PROBLEM ONE
Estimating for a Custom Spread Using 48-inch Fabric

This illustrated example shows how to figure yardage for a quilted filled bedspread for a standard full-size bed of 54 x 75 inches using 48-inch fabric.

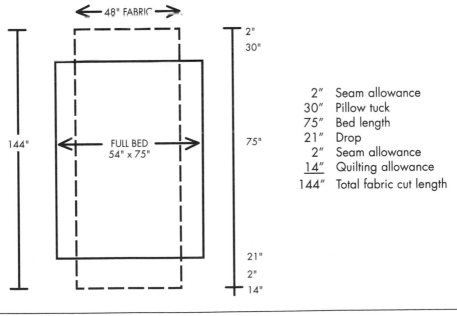

2″	Seam allowance
30″	Pillow tuck
75″	Bed length
21″	Drop
2″	Seam allowance
14″	Quilting allowance
144″	Total fabric cut length

The bed length is 75 inches; the pillow tuck needs 30 inches of fabric; the drop from any side is 21 inches; and 4 inches are needed for the seam allowances, and 14 inches for the quilting allowance (14 inches quilting is just slightly over 10 percent of the total fabric length and is a safe allowance amount). The total length of fabric needed for this spread is 144 inches.

The first length of fabric is always centered down the middle of the bed. Since the fabric is only 48 inches wide, there is a total of 6 inches not covered on the top of the bed by the first piece of fabric.

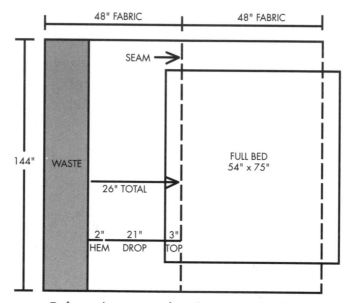

To figure the amount of yardage on each side of the bedspread, you need to add the 3 inches that are not covered on each side on the top of the bed, the 21-inch drop, and the 2-inch seam allowance for a total of 26 inches on each side.

  3″ Left uncovered on one side of bed
21″ Drop
 2″ Seam allowance
26″ Total width for one side of bedspread

Because 26 is more than half of 48, the 48-inch fabric cannot be split in half to use on each side of the bedspread. So a full width of 48-inch fabric will have to be used on the top and each side, requiring three full lengths of fabric. Hopefully the leftover fabric can be used for another part of the bed coverings.

There are three widths of 48-inch fabric needed to cover a full-size bedspread.

First width   48" x 144"
Second width   48" x 144"
Third width   <u>48" x 144"</u>
                        432"

Total length of 432 inches of fabric divided by 36 equals 12 yards.

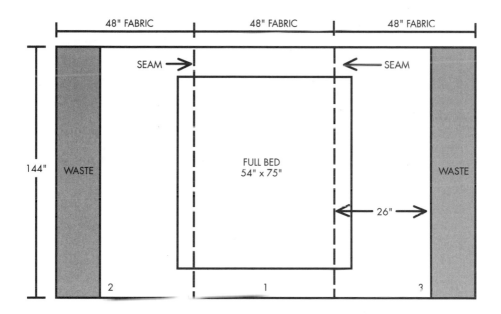

2"	Seam allowance	
30"	Pillow tuck	
75"	Bed length	
21"	Drop	
2"	Seam allowance	
<u>14"</u>	Quilting allowance	
144"	Total fabric cut length x 3	

PROBLEM TWO
Estimating for a Custom Spread Using 54-inch Fabric

This example will show how to figure yardage for a quilted throw bedspread for a full-size bed of 54 x 75 inches using 54-inch-wide fabric.

The length of the bed is 75 inches. The pillow tuck always needs 30 inches of fabric; the bed length is 75 inches; the drop from any side is 21 inches; 4 inches is needed for the seam allowances; and 14 inches for the quilting allowance for a total fabric length of 144 inches.

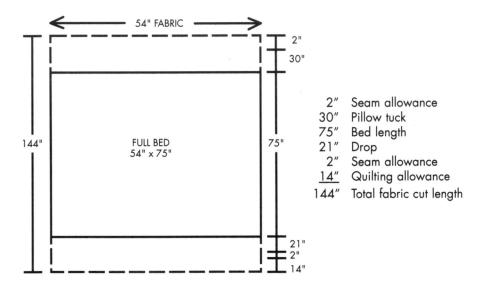

2″	Seam allowance
30″	Pillow tuck
75″	Bed length
21″	Drop
2″	Seam allowance
14″	Quilting allowance
144″	Total fabric cut length

The first length of fabric is always centered down the middle of the bed. Since the bed is 54 inches wide and the fabric is 54 inches wide, the top is completely covered and only the sides need additional material. Each side needs 21 inches for the drop, 2 inches for the seam allowance for a total of 23 inches. Because 23 is less than half of 54, a second piece of fabric can be split in half to use on the sides.

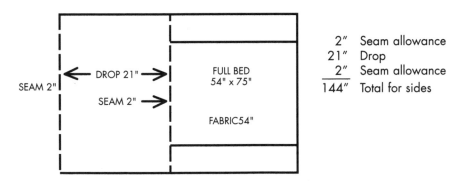

2″	Seam allowance
21″	Drop
2″	Seam allowance
144″	Total for sides

Split in half, each side of the full bedspread can use one length of fabric 144 inches long.

First width   54" x 144"
Second width   <u>54" x 144"</u>
                    288"

Total length of 288 inches of fabric divided by 36 equals 8 yards.

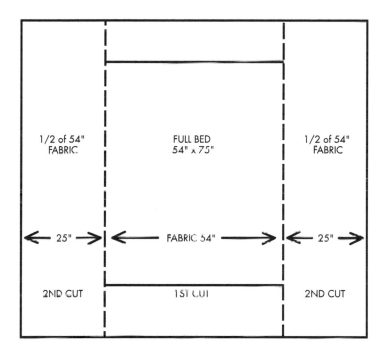

                2"   Hem
               30"   Pillow tuck
               75"   Bed
               21"   Drop
                2"   Hem
              <u>14"</u>   Quilting allowance
              144"   Total

Atypical Beds. Today's need for space and convenience has prompted the design of several other bed styles. One of these beds is the trundle bed or day bed, a spacesaving bed for smaller rooms. This bed is actually two beds; the second bed rolls out from under the top bed. Trundle beds first became popular at the turn of the century when families were large and bed space was limited. Today's trundle beds almost always need custom fitted bedspreads.

To estimate for a custom day-bed comforter, measure the top length of the bed plus two drops of 14 inches each. Most day beds use twin beds, which are 36 inches wide; therefore, either a 48- or 54-inch-wide fabric would be wide enough for the comforter top. Dusters for a day bed are estimated by measuring the two ends and front length, then dividing by the fabric width. Next, multiply by the drop measurement and divide by 36 to get the total yardage, the amount should be doubled for a gathered duster. (See example for fitted duster on page 125.)

Bunk beds are also layered on top of each other, but in many possible configurations and with much more space between each bed than with trundle beds. Children's natural spirit of adventure and agility make bunk beds very popular juvenile furniture. Adventurous custom spreads are common. To estimate for custom twin bedspreads for bunk beds, see the example for a full bed and adjust for twin bed measurements.

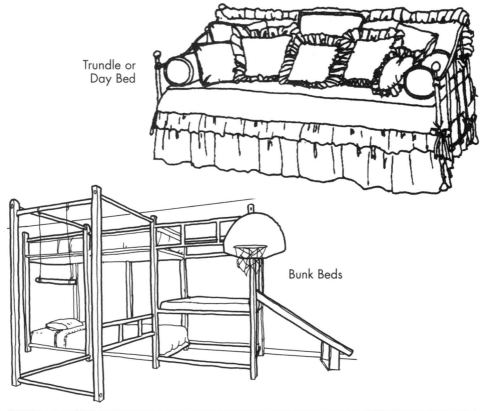

Trundle or
Day Bed

Bunk Beds

A novel and unique bed is the round bed. Seven- and eight-foot-diameter beds are typical and bedspreads for either must be custom measured and made. To estimate for a custom round bedspread, see example for full bedspread and adjust the measurements of the round bed.

Newest to the history of beds is the waterbed. The waterbed is constructed of a solid, rectangular wooden frame with a watertight plastic liner that protects against sudden floods. The mattress is a heavy-duty plastic water bag that has a special heating pad to warm the water to the desired temperature. Many waterbeds need custom bedspreads and comforters. To estimate for a custom waterbed, see the example for estimating a full bedspread and adjust the measurements for the waterbed.

The most customized bed is the built-in bed. All types of conveniences are only an arm's length away. Special lighting, stereo equipment, an alarm system, closed circuit TV, book storage, and clothing storage can all be customized into built-in bed units.

California King bed, 54" plain fabric, throw style*

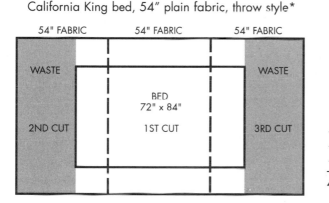

2"	Seam
30"	Pillow tuck
84"	Bed length
21"	Drop
2"	Seam
14"	Quilting allowance
153"	First cut
153"	Second cut
153"	Third cut
459"	Total

$$\frac{12.7 = 13 \text{ yards}}{36\overline{)459}}$$

Full-size bed, 54" plain fabric, throw style*

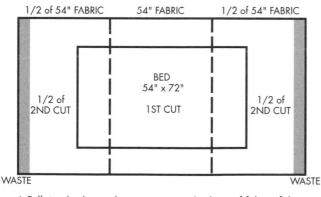

2"	Seam
30"	Pillow tuck
72"	Bed length
21"	Drop
2"	Seam
14"	Quilting allowance
141"	First cut
141"	Second cut
282"	Total

$$\frac{7.8 = 8 \text{ yards}}{36\overline{)282}}$$

* Full-size bedspreads can go into a third cut of fabric if there is a large repeat, wide salvages, or a large quilting pattern

Yardage Chart. The following yardage chart was compiled after consulting with five different custom bedspread workrooms. Three out of five workrooms said it was a good idea to order an extra yard of fabric in case of error.

YARDAGE CHART FOR BEDCOVERINGS

Bedspreads:

Standard Beds			Fabric Width 36" Plain / Repeat	48" Plain / Repeat	54" Plain / Repeat
39" x 75"	Twin	21" drop	12 yards / +2	8 yards / +1	8 yards / +1
54" x 75"	Full	21" drop	12 yards / +2	12 yards / +1	8 yards / +1
60" x 80"	Queen	21" drop	16 yards / +3	13 yards / +2	9 yards / +2
72" x 84"	California King	21" drop	16 yards / +3	13 yards / +2	13 yards / +2
78" x 75"	Dual	21" drop	16 yards / +3	13 yards / +3	13 yards / +2
78" x 80"	Dual King	21" drop	16 yards / +3	13 yards / +3	13 yards / +2
7' x 8'	Round (made to custom measurements)				

Always check king-size measurements, as you can see there are three sizes.

Coverlets:

Standard Beds			Fabric Width 36" Plain / Repeat	48" Plain / Repeat	54" Plain / Repeat
39" x 75"	Twin	12" drop	12 yards / +2	8 yards / +1	8 yards / +1
54" x 75"	Full	12" drop	12 yards / +2	12 yards / +1	8 yards / +1
60" x 80"	Queen	12" drop	15 yards / +2	12 yards / +2	9 yards / +2
72" x 84"	California King	12" drop	15 yards / +3	12 yards / +2	12 yards / +2
78" x 75"	Dual	12" drop	15 yards / +3	12 yards / +2	12 yards / +2
78" x 80"	Dual King	12" drop	15 yards / +3	12 yards / +2	12 yards / +2
7' x 8'	Round (made to custom measurements)				

The cuts of fabric call for the same amount of yardage with about ½–¾ yardage waste from the sides for coverlets.

Yardage includes 30-inch pillow tuck. If no pillow tuck is used, subtract 2 yards.

Comforters:

				Fabric Width		
				36"	48"	54"
Standard Sizes Finished				Plain / Repeat	Plain / Repeat	Plain / Repeat
64" x 88"	Twin	12" drop		9 yards / +2	6 yards / +1	6 yards / +1
78" x 88"	Full	12" drop		9 yards / +2	6 yards / +1	6 yards / +1
84" x 92"	Queen	12" drop		9 yards / +2	9 yards / +2	6 yards / +1
96" x 96"	King	12" drop		13 yards / +3	10 yards / +2	10 yards / +2
102" x 88"	Dual	12" drop		13 yards / +3	10 yards / +2	10 yards / +2
102" x 92"	Dual King	12" drop		13 yards / +3	10 yards / +2	10 yards / +2

Double the yardage for a reversible comforter.

Dust Ruffles/Bed Skirts: 14" Drop

Tailored	36"	48"	54"
Twin	4 yards	3 yards	3 yards
Full	4 yards	3 yards	3 yards
Queen	4½ yards	3 yards	3 yards
King	4½ yards	3½ yards	3½ yards
Dual	4½ yards	3½ yards	3½ yards
Dual King	4½ yards	3½ yards	3½ yards

Shirred or Gathered	36"	48"	54"
Twin	7 yards	5 yards	5 yards
Full	7 yards	6 yards	5 yards
Queen	8 yards	6 yards	6 yards
King	9 yards	7 yards	6 yards
Dual	9 yards	7 yards	6 yards
Dual King	9½ yards	7 yards	7 yards

4" Box Pleated	36"	48"	54"
Twin	9 yards	7 yards	6 yards
Full	9 yards	7 yards	7 yards
Queen	10 yards	8 yards	7 yards
King	11 yards	8 yards	8 yards
Dual	11 yards	8 yards	8 yards
Dual King	11 yards	9 yards	8 yards

	Fabric Width		
Reverse Shams	36"	48"	54"
Twin	3 yards	2 yards	2 yards
Full	3 yards	3 yards	2 yards
Queen	4 yards	3 yards	3 yards
(All) Kings	4 yards	3 yards	3 yards

Bolsters: Round, Wedged, or Rectangular

Fabric Width

	36"	48"	54"
30"–36"	1½ yards	1½ yards	1 yard
39"	2 yards	1½ yards	1 yard
60"	2 yards	2 yards	2 yards
72"	2½ yards	2 yards	2 yards

Jumbo Welting: For Bedspreads, Coverlets, or Comforters

	36"	48"	54"
1"–2" diameter cord	2 yards	2 yards	1½ yards

Top Welting: For Bedspreads & Coverlets

	36"	48"	54"
Regular cord	2 yards	2 yards	1½ yards

Pillow Shams:

		36"	48"	54"
Standard	20" x 30"	2 yards	2 yards	3 yards
King	20" x 36"	2 yards	2 yards	3½ yards
Queen	20" x 20"	2 yards	2 yards	3 yards

Throw Pillows:

	Body of Pillow	1st Ruffle or Flap	Accent Welt
12" x 12"	½ yard	⅔ yard	⅓ yard
16" x 16"	½ yards	1 yards	½ yard
20" x 20"	1 yard	1 yard	½ yards
30" x 30"	2 yards	1½ yards	⅔ yard

COST ESTIMATING

When estimating costs for bed coverings, there will be one labor cost to make bedspreads, dusters, pillows, and so forth, and one material cost for the fabrics and trims. The labor and material costs will always be changing as new products are introduced and prices increase. Designer sheets, such as Ralph Lauren, are about three times the price of regular fabric yardage, a very expensive way to go.

TIME ESTIMATING

To begin the work, send the filled-out work order to the workroom, keeping a copy for reference. The work order can be faxed or mailed out the day you get the signed contract and a 50 percent deposit (most workrooms require a 50 percent deposit with a work order). Next, you need to order the fabric. Most fabric companies will send you or the workroom in-stock yardage within two to six days, depending on how far away the fabric company is located. They can have it shipped in two days if you are willing to pay for red- or blue-label express service.

If the fabric is back-ordered, your order could be delayed. (Back orders are common, especially on popular prints or colors. They represent one of the major headaches of interior design.) If the fabric is back-ordered, the fabric company will give you an estimated shipping date. (A fabric can be back-ordered several times before it is actually shipped.) The proper thing to do is to notify the client immediately and let him or her know of the delay. He or she may elect to wait it out, to choose a different fabric, or to cancel the order.

Assuming all fabrics are "good in stock" and can be shipped to the workroom within five days, the next step is fabricating the order. Most bedspread workrooms will take approximately two to three weeks to cut and quilt the fabric and add any detailing trim. When the order is ready, the workroom will either notify you to pick it up or ship it to you via UPS, which will add another two to three days to the process. The time from receiving the order to delivering the finished bedcovering(s) to the client, can take from three to six weeks.

CHOOSING A BED COVERING WORK ROOM

When choosing a workroom to make custom bedcoverings, make sure they have a standard procedure of inspecting your fabric before cutting it. This is critical, as no fabric company will accept returned goods that have been cut. It is also the responsibility of the designer to inspect the goods before they are fabricated. Keep in mind that some fabrics, including woven silks, silk-screened prints, and nubby cotton prints, have irregularities by nature. Both linen and chintz-finished cottons, for example, will often have wrinkles that will not smooth out. Make sure to explain this to the client well in advance.

Never assume the expertise of a bedspread workroom. Ask for references and always pay a visit in person to inspect their procedures. Observe the work in progress and their finished goods. Check out the quilting details and look at finished seams and edges. Ask about detailed work or unusual items they can make. Have them show you the size welts they use and the different fillings they stock. Request a price list and read it over, asking questions. Never assume that the workroom knows what you mean; always get a signed work order. This will prevent misunderstandings and, when problems do arise, help to determine who is responsible for the repairs.

In addition, some bedcovering workrooms have the machinery and skilled workers to fabricate both draperies and bed coverings. It is more convenient to use a workroom that provides both services; if you use two separate workrooms, then fabrics have to be ordered together and sent to two different locations.

EXAMPLE OF FINAL BEDCOVERING COSTS

Mr. and Mrs. Bennett hired an interior designer to design unique and customized bed coverings for their master bedroom. They wanted a lightweight comforter, a gathered dust ruffle, four pillow shams with contrast welting, and several 16" x 16" decorative pillows. They chose two fabrics, both 54 inches wide, one solid-colored and the other a flower print with a 25-inch repeat.

Measurements
King-size bed: 72" x 80" with a 14" drop
King-size shams: 20" x 36" each, two with contrasting welt
Decorative pillows: 16" x 16" each

According to the yardage chart on page 138, a comforter of these measurements would require 12 yards of fabric with 1/2 yard extra for quilting allowance; a king-size gathered dust ruffle would require 6 yards; four king-size pillows would require 6 yards of fabric; and three 16" x 16" decorative pillows would require 4½ yards of fabric.

After you have completed all the measuring, calculating and estimating, present the final figures to the client on a contract. The final figures for the master bedroom would look something like this:

Labor: Comforter–King size with 6-oz. filling, pattern quilted $150.00
Fabric: Pattern–Trillium; color–cornsilk; 12½ yards @ $43.00   541.80
         (1/2 yard is needed for shrinkage when quilting)

Labor: Dust ruffle–king size, gathered, self-lined   90.00
Fabric: Pattern–crushed silk; color–cream; 6 yards @ $19. 95   119.70

Labor: 2 king pillow shams, double ruffled, shirred welt @ $38.00 each   76.00
        2 standard pillow shams, single ruffle, fringe @ $40.00 ea.   80.00
Fabric: Pattern–Trillium; color–cornsilk; 3 yards @ $43.00   129.00
        Pattern–crushed silk; color–cream; 3 yards @ $19.95   59.85

Labor: 2 standard pillows, 16" x 16", fringed @ $10.00   30.00
Fabric: Pattern–Flora; color–cream; 2½ yards @ 32.00   83.20
        Fringe–French, color–multi-gold; 4½ yards @ $15.95   71.80

                             Subtotal $1,431.35
                          Tax 6.5% **   107.35
                                 TOTAL $1,538.70

Estimated time to fabricate: three to six weeks after receipt of all fabrics at work-room.

  * All figures are based on 2001 Phoenix, Arizona prices.
 ** Each state would calculate tax differently according to their state laws: Some states apply tax on newly manufactured products only. (Bed coverings are considered new products and labor is included.) Check your state laws to see what sale and use taxes apply.

This elegant, chenille-welt-trimmed coverlet is a historical reproduction from the Hearst Castle. The bed skirt and pillows are designed with crushed silk, and the curved headboard is covered in tiny-striped silk.

Bedcovering Work Order

Date: March 10, 2001
P.O. # 1201
Designer: Carol Sampson
Address: 7601 Scottsdale Rd.
Scottsdale, AZ
Phone: (480) 956-5656

Installation
Address:

Date Fabric Received: March 10, 2001
Date Promised: April 9, 2001
Workroom: Evelyn's Drapery
Address: 1234 White Road
Scottsdale, AZ
Phone: (480) 989-5506

Mr. & Mrs. J. Bennett
4300 Gainey Ranch
Scottsdale, AZ
(480) 905-5777

Bedspread Style	Quilting Pattern	No Tuck	No Sham	Width	Length	Drop	Fabric Co.	Color	Pattern	Fabric Width	Repeat
Pillow Tuck / Reverse Sham											

Comforter Style	Quilting Pattern	Width	Length	Drop	Fabric Co.	Color	Pattern	Fabric Width	Repeat
1. Coverlet Style King throw		84" *(finished size)*	96"	12"	Pindler + Pindler	Cornsilk	Trillium	54"	12"
2. Dust Ruffle Style Gathered		King	King	14"	Pindler + Pindler	Cream	Crushed Silk	54"	0

Pillow Sham Style	Quilting Pattern	Width	Length	Quantity	Fabric Co.	Color	Pattern	Fabric Width	Repeat
3. 2-King	0	36"	20"	2	Pindler + Pindler	Cornsilk	Trillium	54"	0
4. 2-Standard		26"	20"	2	Pindler + Pindler	Cream	Crushed Silk	54"	0
5. Custom Pillows	0	16"	16"	3	P.+P.	Musti gold	Travel	54"	0

Special Instructions:
2 – King Shams – double ruffled w/ slivered welt
2 – Standard Shams – single ruffle, fringed
3 – Decorator Pillows – Trimmed with fringe

P.S. Please return all fabric & left over trims.
Any questions, please call me.

Bedcovering Work Order

Date: _____

P.O. #: _____

Designer: _____

Address: _____

Phone: _____

Installation

Address: _____

Phone: _____

Date Fabric Received: _____

Date Promised: _____

Workroom: _____

Address: _____

Phone: _____

Bedspread Style		Quilting Pattern		Width	Length	Drop	Fabric Co.	Color	Pattern	Fabric Width	Repeat
Pillow Tuck	Reverse Sham	No Tuck	No Sham								

Comforter Style	Quilting Pattern	Width	Length	Drop	Fabric Co.	Color	Pattern	Fabric Width	Repeat

Coverlet Style

Dust Ruffle Style

Pillow Sham Style	Quilting Pattern	Width	Length	Quantity	Fabric Co.	Color	Pattern	Fabric Width	Repeat

Custom Pillows

Special Instructions:

Chapter Six
TABLECLOTHS

Multi-layered and multi-trimmed tablecloth.

Tablecloth tables have become a valuable interior design tool and many have been elevated to works of art when the fabrics and trims used are elaborate, rich and elegant materials. This table treatment is new in the history of design, it has only been used over the last century. Tablecloth tables first found their way into the bedroom during the twenties as a dressing or vanity table for ladies to apply and display various makeup, perfumes and accessories. These early vanity tablecloths had full linings and dressmaker touches like pleats and welting with fabrics designed to look like a fine pair of draperies. Today's ladies still make use of this tablecloth table and dress it up to reflect their personalities . The area under the table's skirt is great for hidden storage space.

Gradually, the tablecloth table idea spread throughout the house, finding practical use in all rooms. They have gained in popularity as a unique way to add style and function to any room.

Many designers use gorgeous tablecloth tables in the living room designed with double and triple layers of fabrics in velvets, silks, rich wovens and tapestries trimmed with fringes, braids, banding or square scarfs. Even using expensive fabrics, the tablecloth table is still less expensive than most end tables.

Dining rooms and breakfast rooms are a natural for the tablecloth table. An expensive fabric below can be covered by a less expensive fabric square and topped with a protective piece of glass for a fraction of the cost of a typical dining table. A selection of different cloths can be interchanged each season for year round variety and special occasions. For example, a solid velvet base fabric in the

Styles

Plain	Ruffled	Jumbo Welt	Fitted Top

| Border | Plain & Short Round | Plain & Square | Rosette |

dining room for more formal occasions could then have a beautiful print square on top that would change and correspond to the holidays; Thanksgiving, Christmas, Easter, etc. Breakfast room tables could have a wardrobe of tablecloths to coordinate with special family events, birthdays, anniversary or parties.

Tablecloth tables come in handy in children's rooms, secondary rooms, quest rooms and dens, where a smaller amount of the decorating budget is spent. The round shape is still the most preferred, but a rectangle shape works well against the wall in living rooms, dining rooms, bedrooms or hallways and can hide a considerable amount of stacked boxes underneath.

Any size circumference or rectangle can be used, depending on the location and tabletop needs. The average size diameter is usually between 30 inches and 42 inches, which is an ideal size for a bedside table, providing enough room for a lamp, alarm clock, reading material, photographs, and other accessories. A smaller top measurement of 24 inches in diameter is large enough to hold a lamp and a few accessories. Larger sizes for the dining room would measure between 60 inches to 72 inches, making sure the under base is strong enough to hold the larger size. Typical rectangle tables can be 30 x 60 or slightly larger at 36 x 72 or customized to fit a particular space.

TABLECLOTH MATERIALS

Because the table itself is concealed by the tablecloth, the framework can be made from pressboard, a folding table, a drop-down table or custom made from rough lumber. Even an old marred table or desk that may be unusable by itself can serve as a base for a tablecloth table. Knocked-down pressboard round versions can be bought in several sizes from lumber companies, bedding stores, discount stores or catalogs.

Tablecloth tables can add a formal or informal design statement to any style or period room setting. They are appropriate in formal surroundings when fabrics such as silks, brocades, velvets, damasks, laces, satins, moires and fine cotton prints or stripes are used. Today, huge selections of elegant trims for formal settings have made choices endless. These include: fringes, braids, French gimp, tassels, cords, banding, ribbons and welting. For informal settings, tablecloth fabrics include patterned cotton prints or stripes, piqué, seersucker, plisse, laces, chintz, linens or textured patterns. Many trims for the informal setting can come from contrasting fabrics and be used as ruffles, banding, jumbo welts, shirred cording, pleats, scalloped edges, borders and rosettes. Unusual heavier fabrics can spark up an informal room by using a quilt for a tablecloth. Most tablecloths should be lined to give them a softer fullness and to prevent light showing through the base of the table, especially if an unattractive base has been used.

MEASURING FOR TABLECLOTHS

Since most fabrics are 48 or 54 inches wide and the diameter of the smallest floor length tablecloth is 84 inches including the 30-inch drop, most tablecloths will need two lengths of fabric to create enough width. Seams must never be put down the middle; they should be placed on both sides equidistant from the center. The first width of fabric is used for the center of the tablecloth and the second width is split in half to be sewn on either side of the center strip.

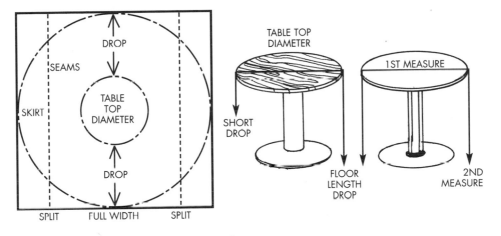

First, measure the tabletop to determine the required diameter of the cloth. Next, measure the length of the drop twice, once for each side, then add 2 inches allowance for seams.

To estimate for a tablecloth pattern repeat, simply add the width of one pattern repeat to the total length of fabric. If you want the pattern to fall in a specific place, such as a bouquet centered on the top or around the sides of the tablecloth, write

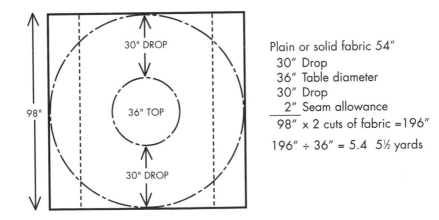

Plain or solid fabric 54"
   30" Drop
   36" Table diameter
   30" Drop
   2" Seam allowance
   98" x 2 cuts of fabric =196"

196" ÷ 36" = 5.4 5½ yards

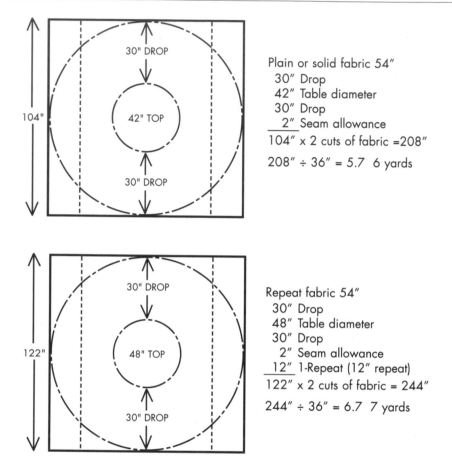

Plain or solid fabric 54"
30" Drop
42" Table diameter
30" Drop
2" Seam allowance
104" x 2 cuts of fabric =208"
208" ÷ 36" = 5.7 6 yards

Repeat fabric 54"
30" Drop
48" Table diameter
30" Drop
2" Seam allowance
12" 1-Repeat (12" repeat)
122" x 2 cuts of fabric = 244"
244" ÷ 36" = 6.7 7 yards

detailed instructions on the work order (it is a good idea to attach a sketch to avoid misunderstandings).

Fitted Tablecloths. Fitted tablecloths can be made for any table. However, you must provide the workroom with a pattern from which to cut the fitted top. To make a pattern, lay brown paper over the tabletop. Firmly holding the paper in place, crease it along the table edges to define the table perimeter, then run the side of a pencil along the table edge.

Tablecloths from Sheets. Tablecloths can also be made from sheets. This is particularly appropriate in a bedroom, where tablecloths sewn from sheets can match an entire bedroom ensemble including bedspread, duster, shams, comforters, and pillows. Most workrooms can fabricate sheets into tablecloths, draperies, pillows, comforters, and so forth.

A queen-size flat sheet can be made into a tablecloth of 82 to 90 inches in diameter. A king-size flat sheet can make a tablecloth of 91 to 102 inches in diameter;

king-size sheets are large enough that there is no need to worry about pattern repeats.

Other Tablecloth Styles. There are various tablecloth styles and treatments, each with a different effect and each with its own estimating requirement. A ruffle of the same fabric or a contrasting one can be added to the plain tablecloth style. Ruffles usually measure anywhere from 3 inches to 15 inches deep, depending on the design. To estimate yardage for a tablecloth ruffle, multiply diameter times pi (3.14) to get the circumference. Example: The tabletop diameter is 42 inches; adding two drops of 30 inches gives you the total diameter of the tablecloth: 104. Multiply 104 inches by 3.14 to get 327 inches, the total diameter of the tablecloth. Next, divide the fabric width of 54 (or 48) into 327 inches to find the number of widths you need (in this case, 6). Finally, decide how deep a ruffle you want (for this problem a 12-inch-wide ruffle is used). Multiply 6 widths times 12 inches equals 72 inches; divide by 36 (one yard) to get 2 yards, and finally, multiply by 2 1/2 to estimate fullness for the ruffle. Your final required yardage is 5 yards.

D π = C	D π = 104 x 3.14 = 327 circumference
Widths	327 ÷ 54 = 6 widths
Width times ruffle depth	6w x 12 = 72
Straight yardage	72 ÷ 36 = 2 yards
Total ruffle yardage	2 x 2½ fullness = 5 yards

Jumbo welts, 1½- or 3-inch round cord covered in the same or contrasting material, come in various sizes and can have fabric shirred or gathered on the welt for a textural effect. Estimate jumbo-welt yardage for contrasting fabric the same way as you would a ruffle, with or without the fullness. Fitted tops can be used on oddly shaped tables, dressing tables, or where the top edge is accented with a decorative trim or welting. Borders around the bottom of the tablecloth can be made from contrasting fabrics, fringe, lace, or ribbons.

To estimate the yardage for a border trim, determine the circumference of the tablecloth using the formula above. Next, divide the circumference by 36 to get the total linear yardage.

A short round tablecloth (usually under 60 inches in diameter) is often used on top of a longer floor-length cloth in a contrasting color or pattern. A square cloth, often lace or embroidery, measuring either 42 x 42 inches or 54 x 54 inches is also used over a floor-length cloth. Rosette tablecloths are often lightweight fabrics and either the workroom or the installer ties the tablecloth to form a rosette.

Yardage Chart. Use the following chart to estimate the yardage needed for plain style tablecloths.

Yardage Chart			
Style	Top Diameter	Drop	54" Yardage
Plain	36	8	2 yards
	36	12	4 yards
	36	18	4 yards
	36	30	6 yards
	42	8	4 yards
	42	12	4 yards
	42	18	5 yards
	42	30	6 yards
	48	8	4 yards
	48	12	4 yards
	48	18	5 yards
	48	30	6.5 yards
	54	8	4 yards
	54	12	5 yards
	54	18	5 yards
	54	30	10 yards

Pattern Repeat: Add one repeat size to total yardage.

COST ESTIMATING

There will be possibly three costs for estimating tablecloths: fabric, trims and labor charges from the workroom. The fabric and trim costs will vary, depending on the selection and layered amounts called for in the design. The tablecloth labor cost is always specified either on the workroom price list or on a visit to personally describe or draw the details. The more elaborate the design, the safer it would be to make a personal visit to insure accuracy to the design.

TIME ESTIMATING

Depending on the detailing required, a workroom usually will take two to three days to fabricate a tablecloth after all fabrics have been received.

CHOOSING A WORKROOM

There are several workrooms that will sew a custom tablecloth, including drapery workrooms, bedcovering workrooms, and independent seamstresses. There are also bedding shops that will custom-sew tablecloths. Tablecloths are fairly easy to make and do not require the same level of expertise as draperies and bedcoverings. The best way to evaluate their work is to check samples and call references of happy, satisfied clients.

EXAMPLE OF FINAL CUSTOM TABLECLOTH COSTS

Mrs. Mulholland has asked her designer to estimate the costs of a tablecloth for her bedroom table. The table has a 42-inch-diameter top and a 30-inch drop. Mrs. Mulholland wants a plain style with a gathered jumbo welt at the hem. The flower-printed fabric she has selected is 54 inches wide with a 22-inch repeat.

Table Measurements
42-inch diameter, with a 30-inch drop.

According to the yardage chart on page 152, a tablecloth of these measurements will require 6 yards. Add 1 yard for the 22-inch pattern repeat for a total of 7 yards.

After you have completed your measuring, calculating, and estimating, present the final figures to the client on a contract. The final figures would look something like this:

Labor: Plain style, 42-inch diameter, 30-inch drop tablecloth
with gathered jumbo welt (welt cord included) $ 30.00

Fabric: Pattern—Bouquet; color—multi; 7 yards @ 49.95   349.65

Subtotal	$ 379.65
Tax 7.4% **	28.47
TOTAL	$408.12

Estimated time to fabricate: two to three weeks after receipt of fabric because most workrooms run two to three weeks ahead on their own scheduling before they take on new work.

 * All figures based on 2001 Arizona prices.
** Each state would calculate tax differently according to their state laws. Some states apply tax on newly manufactured products only. Bed coverings are considered a new product, therefore this labor is taxed. Check your state laws to see what sale and use taxes apply.

Tablecloth Work Order

Date: May 4, 2001

P.O. # 1595

Designer: Carol Sawyer

Address: 7601 Scottsdale Rd
Scottsdale, AZ

Phone: (480) 956-5656

Address:

Drapery
Workroom: Point Custom Drapery

Address: 6800 19th Street
Costa Mesa, Ca.

Phone: (909) 986-6555

Customer info:
Mrs. Mulholland
147 No. Grove
Newport, Ca.
(909) 883-4567

Tablecloth Fabric & Color	Yards	Plain Round	Style Fitted Top	Other	Total Finished Size	Finished Drop	Hem Size
Banquet 1. Color-Multi'	7	X			D-102" Repeat 22"	30"	4"
2.							
3.							

Fancy Work	Yards	Trim Size	Trim Color	Trim Fabric	Ruffle Depth	Size 1" or 2"	Jumbo Welt Straight	Shirred Gathered
1. HEM		Same as Tablecloth				2"		X
2.								
3.								

Instructions: Center largest flower bouquet just above hem line.

Drawing:

Tablecloth Work Order

Date: _____

P.O. # _____

Designer: _____

Address: _____

Phone: _____

Address: _____

Phone: _____

Drapery _____

Workroom: _____

Address: _____

Phone: _____

Tablecloth Fabric & Color	Yards	Plain Round	Style Fitted Top	Other	Total Finished Size			Finished Drop	Hem Size
1.									
2.									
3.									

Fancy Work	Yards	Trim Size	Trim Color	Trim Fabric	Ruffle Depth	Size 1" or 2"	Jumbo Welt Straight	Shirred Gathered
1.								
2.								
3.								

Instructions:

Drawing:

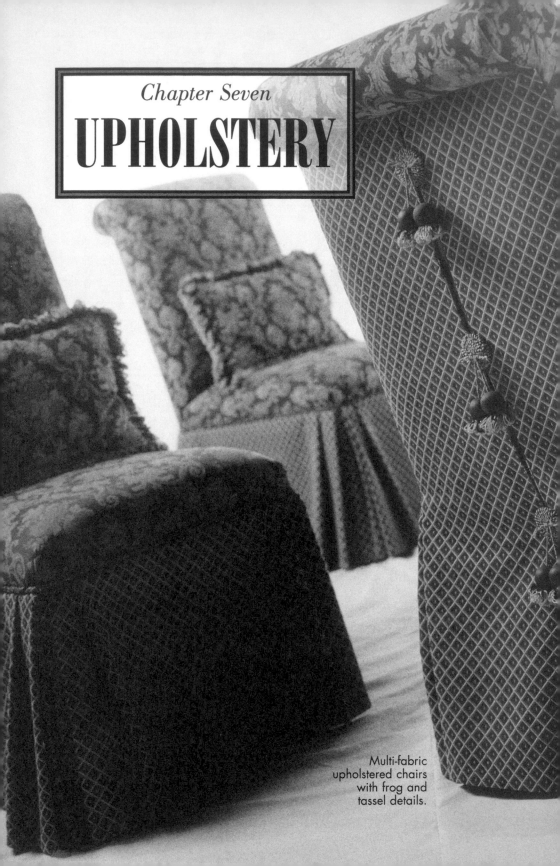

Multi-fabric
upholstered chairs
with frog and
tassel details.

Upholstered furniture first appeared during the Renaissance in France and Italy. The practice of using cushions on the seats of wood chairs gradually led to integrating seat and back cushions with the frame to prevent the loose cushions from slipping.

The first completely upholstered chair was introduced in France in the middle of the nineteenth century. These chairs were so plush that they were called comfortables. The fully upholstered chair gradually developed into the chaise for a semireclining position. The rest of Europe quickly adopted this new enhancement to their interiors.

Down, feathers, horse hair, cotton, and burlap were used as construction materials for upholstery until the 1940s. After World War II, natural materials for upholstery were put aside in favor of the new, less expensive synthetics like polyfill, polyester, and Dacron. Today, both natural and synthetic fibers are used for upholstery construction. The most expensive chairs and sofas still have goose down and feathers in their cushions.

UPHOLSTERY BASICS

Upholstery is the end result of covering and stuffing the wood frame of a sofa, chair, or any padded seating unit. Many design projects will require some upholstery to be purchased or redone. Accordingly, every designer should have a sound knowledge of the materials available and the comfort levels required. Materials will include any type of exterior decorative cover and trim; interior cushioning and wrap; support springs and strapping; plus the basic wooden structural framework. Comfort levels will include soft, medium, firm, and extra firm. The designer's service to a client should not only guarantee good design, but the comfort and durability of their upholstery as well.

There are three types of upholstery: custom-made, ready-made, and reupholstered.

Custom-made. Custom-made upholstery is a one-of-a-kind piece of upholstered furniture made to specific size, dimension, and design to meet individual designer/client requirements. This upholstery uses the best materials, such as a strong wood frame in a medium-dense wood, coiled eight-way hand-tied springs, cushions filled with goose down and feathers, jute strapping, foam padding, and a muslin cover. The furniture is made to specific requirements and is therefore very expensive. However, an expensively made custom piece will last many lifetimes; only the exterior fabric will need changing through the years.

Ready-made. Ready-made upholstery is manufactured in large quantities to regulated sizes, dimensions, and designs to meet the needs of the general public. Ready-made pieces will range in price and quality from the very expensive to the very inexpensive. A top-quality line of ready-made upholstery can be as good as custom-made. Many high-end furniture manufacturers have solid reputations based on their ready-made stock. In addition, many manufacturers can customize any sofa, chair, or ottoman in their line. This would include providing custom sizes, extra pillows, quilting, down cushions, arm caps, contrast fabrics, double welting, stylized skirts, and sleeper units.

At the opposite end, cheap ready-made furniture is easy to find. These manufacturers advertise 100 percent nonsag construction, which often consists of zigzag bent-wire springs with no support webbing for the seating base. This seating will give out in a few years of normal wear. Cheap wood frames are stapled together and can easily start squeaking or come apart. Their cushions are inexpensive foam designed for looks rather than durability. The best location for cheap ready-made upholstery is in model homes where the upholstery pieces are just for show

Reupholstery . Reupholstering the existing upholstered sofa, loveseat, chair, chaises, ottoman, etc. may be cost effective and save money if the piece to be re-covered was originally well made. The cost to reupholster will hinge mostly on the fabric selection. The cost of an inexpensive canvas versus an expensive, washed chenille can be enormous and push the price to reupholster close to the purchase price of a brand new piece of furniture.

An unknown cost to reupholster will be to what degree the piece needs repairs or reconstruction. There are many questions that need to be addressed. Is the frame loose or broken and in need of repair? Are the eight way hand-tied inner springs in need of re-tying or replacement? Are the inner cushions broken down or lumpy and need replacement? Is any of the exposed wood scratched or dented and in need of refinishing? Does the swivel rocker need new hardware? Does the old upholstery have good inner structure but needs updating or re-styling of the frame, legs or outside cover? Answers to these questions will determine whether or not to reupholster or buy new.

MATERIAL ESTIMATING

Upholstery fabrics come in a wide variety ranging from heavy textured cottons and wools to delicate silks. These fabrics can be imported or domestically made and have a broad range of quality and price. The most common fabric widths are 48 or 54 inches.

Construction Basics. It is important to have an understanding of the basics of upholstery construction, as different variables will affect your measuring and estimating as well as many of your design decisions.

The basic parts of an upholstered piece of furniture are the frame, the webbing, the springs, the filling, the cushions, the decorative outer covering, and some kind of detailing. These are shown in the figure opposite.

Frames. The frame is the skeleton of any upholstery piece and supports not oniy the rest of the upholstery, but the occupant as well. American kiln-dried hardwoods are preferred for expensive, high-end furniture. The lumber is placed in a

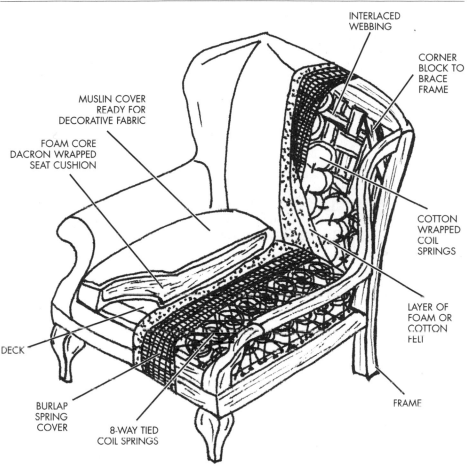

INTERLACED WEBBING

CORNER BLOCK TO BRACE FRAME

MUSLIN COVER READY FOR DECORATIVE FABRIC

FOAM CORE DACRON WRAPPED SEAT CUSHION

COTTON WRAPPED COIL SPRINGS

LAYER OF FOAM OR COTTON FELT

DECK

FRAME

BURLAP SPRING COVER

8-WAY TIED COIL SPRINGS

dry kiln under controlled humidity and heat conditions to remove excess moisture and to prevent future warping. A quality frame in any upholstered piece shouldn't have any creaking sounds, or wobble when moved or sat on. Quality wooden frames use lumber that is large scale in dimensions and cut and shaped to the contour of each style. Outside corners on the frame should be beveled to prevent fabric wear especially on the outside leg and arm areas. The best interior wood frames are birch, poplar, maple, gum, sycamore, and elm. Exposed carved wood frames can be made of more expensive woods such as mahogany, pecan or walnut and most imported frames are made of a varity of exotic woods.

Frame joints need to be put together like a jigsaw puzzle, reinforcing the corners with corner blocks attached with wood glue and double-dowel screws for durability and rigidity. The inexpensive upholstery products can cost less because of inferior frame pieces that are stapled or nailed together, and which can loosen eventually and come apart.

Webbing. Webbing is a taut strapping used as a foundation to support seats, backs, and arms. Webbing should be 3½- to 4-inches-wide nylon, jute or polypropylene straps interlaced and stretched taught on the frame to support the springs. Support webbing isn't often used under inexpensive upholstery pieces because it will result in sagging of the seat cushions.

Springs. Springs are the inner foundation for seats and backs, and are made in either coil or nonsag construction. They are one of the most important components in any upholstered piece of furniture. The main differences between coil or nonsag springs are construction, price and comfort.

The better manufacturers and upholstery shops use the nonrusting, tempered steel coil or cone shaped springs. When used in a seat, they are closely placed together and firmly anchored, then hand tied with strong twine in eight ways; four across and four diagonal. The twine is next securely fastened to the frame rails. High-end upholstery will often display a tag saying, "eight-way hand tied" to announce their high quality. The extra labor and time required to tie coil springs increases the cost of fine upholstery.

Not only are coil springs more durable, but they also are more comfortable. Coil springs are resilient, easily springing down and back with every sitting while continuing to support the seated person.

When used in a back, a lighter weight coil spring is muslin or cotton pocket-wrapped and then stapled together four ways. This forms a firm comfortable back support. Whether seat or back cushions, you should never feel the springs or hear any thumps or squeaking.

Less expensive nonsag springs are "S" shaped, flat 2½ to 3 feet lengths of high-grade tempered steel. They are stapled at each end to the frame. Nonsag spring units are more rigid and less comfortable. Much less time and effort is required to install these. And finally, the non-sag spring construction will not wear over the long run as will the coil spring units.

Filling. After the springs are installed, they are covered with several layers of filling or padding to separate the springs from the cushions and prevent pokes. The first layer can be a ten-ounce piece of burlap or a nonabsorbent, odor-free foam or polypropylene sheeting that comes in soft, medium or firm densities. The next layer is either cotton batting or a fluffy polyester fiber filling. The last layer is canvas, muslin or sateen fabric that becomes the seat decking which supports the seat cushion. In quality pieces, the decking is made from the decorative fabric used to cover the exterior upholstery. In the past, some antique upholstery had fillings that would cause problems. Fillings such as moss, kapok, sisal, tow, excelsior and seaweed are no longer used because they cause unwanted smells, mildew, mold, bugs and can be flammable. Muslin is placed on top of the padding to cover all structural upholstered areas and acts like a lining before the finish or decorative fabric is applied..

Cushions. Cushions for upholstery are removable, separate forms for seats and backs that are shaped to fit the desired design of the upholstery style. There are several different cushion constructions available for both the seats and backs to give choices in levels of comfort and in price range.

Most standard seat and back cushions have a core of polyurethane foam in various densities from soft, medium and high resiliency and can have up to three wraps in other materials, such as polyester fiber, cotton batting or down. This type of cushion has a high or soft resiliency polyurethane foam core and is wrapped on top, front edge and bottom with polyester fiber or cotton batting that is glued to the core. The core and wrap are then inserted into a sewn casing of cotton muslin or nonwoven polyester and then the unit is ready for muslin or nonwoven polyester and then the unit is ready for the outer decorative finish fabric.

The more expensive back and seat cushions focus on a higher comfort level that translates into coil springs and up to five wraps. This type of cushion has an inner core of tempered steel coil springs pocket-wrapped in muslin, which is mounted

Structure of Cushions

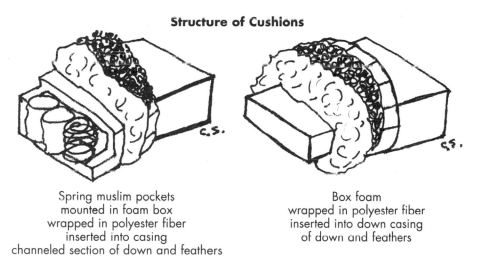

| Spring muslin pockets mounted in foam box wrapped in polyester fiber inserted into casing channeled section of down and feathers | Box foam wrapped in polyester fiber inserted into down casing of down and feathers |

into a fabricated box of polyurethane foam. This unit is wrapped in polyester fiber and inserted into a channeled down-proof muslin casing. The casing has sewn dividers to form channels which prevents the down filling from shifting in use. The down filling is made up of different combinations and percentages of polyester fiber, waterfowl feathers and white duck down. Typical combinations would be 50% polyester fiber, 35% waterfowl feathers and 15% white duck down. The combination of coil spring, polyester fiber and down helps the cushion maintain it's shape while still being extremely comfortable.

Seat and back cushions should have a slight crown; that is, the center of a cushion should be higher than its outside perimeter. To achieve this, the inner cushion should be about four inches until it is inserted inside the decorative finish fabric and pulled tightly down at the edges to about three inches, leaving the center with a slightly higher crown.

When upholstering with cotton prints you should make sure that the cotton can't be seen through into the inner construction, where unwanted seams or wraps may show. In European upholstery shops, they use a liner of flannel to prevent this from happening, especially on the inside back, cushion deck and all around the skirt where light may show through.

Coverings. The decorative, exterior, outside fabric covering will be the most visible part of the upholstered furniture. This covering can be selected from a wide range of materials—woven textures, cotton prints, wools, silks, and a variety of blends—depending on the design concept and the budget of the client. Most upholstery fabrics are 54 inches wide, with a few cottons in 48-inch widths.

Fabrics can be put on the upholstered piece in one of two ways, either "as woven" or railroaded. Railroading means running the fabric horizontally along the width of an upholstered piece of furniture. Railroading fabrics usually costs much less to upholster because there is less piecing and cutting of the fabric.

Railroading a fabric horizontally on the upholstery uses a little less yardage than upholstering a fabric vertically. Railroading a fabric is not possible when there is a pattern repeat because the pattern would be on its side. Stripes have tra-

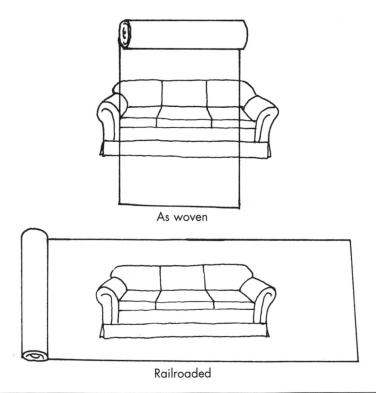

As woven

Railroaded

ditionally been applied to upholstery pieces only in a vertical manner and look awful railroaded on the horizontals.

Detailing. Some type of finish material is always needed to hide the raw edges of the fabric, where it meets the exposed wood frame, to cover tacks, and to highlight the custom craftsmanship put into the upholstered piece. These materials can be a decorative element adding to the finished beauty of the upholstery. Some of the materials available for detailing include welting, buttons, nail heads, cording, braids, fringes, tassels, and gimps. Cord welting can be of the same fabric as the upholstery, a contrasting fabric, or even a coordinating fabric, such as a stripe welt on a printed upholstery fabric. Either a single or double welt can be appropriate for many traditional or contemporary styles of upholstery. Quite often several are combined for more elaborately designed upholstered pieces.

Channeling or tufting can be done to the back. Channeling runs straight from the top of the chair or sofa back down to the seat cushion. A channel-back is used instead of a back cushion. Tufting has deep folds of fabric laid out in a diamond design, then pushed into the back of an upholstered piece and secured with a button. Another way to detail is at the skirt or flounce. These are fabric panels surrounding the base of a chair, sofa, or chaise that reach to the floor and hide the furniture legs. Skirts or flounces can be flat, ruffled, box pleated, shirred, gathered at corners, or trimmed with deep fringes.

Another very important finishing detail is the protection of the final fabric from soiling and stains. Fabric-protection chemicals can be sprayed onto any upholstered piece. Treatments are on the market to protect fabrics in both natural or synthetic fibers. The small cost of fabric protection far outweighs the cost of having upholstery recovered. Another way to protect upholstery is to specify arm covers or caps. These will give added protection to areas that are constantly being handled; they are an inexpensive investment to protect an area of high use.

Extras. Extras are always in addition to the regular labor charges. Pattern matching fabric repeats always adds extra labor time and charges to every piece of upholstered furniture. Pillows in contrasting decorative fabrics and various sizes may be an added extra that makes a design statement you want. Metal castors for the bottom of legs can be a welcome extra for a safer and more efficient way to move chairs or heavier upholstery around. Pick up and delivery charges along with installation charges (headboards, beds, cornices) are sometimes necessary extras if you don't have the manpower and a large enough vehicle to transport the items. If the client's home is out of town or out of state from the upholstery shop, an extra charge could be for packing and shipping to a distant location.

HOW TO MEASURE AND ESTIMATE FOR UPHOLSTERY

There are two ways to estimate upholstery: by using an upholstery chart or by measuring and laying out each section of the furniture piece. Most charts have an illustration and the yardage needed printed under the picture. There are many charts available through upholstery shops; however, they should only be used for "guesstimates." They can vary in the correct yardage needed by up to two yards, because they do not correspond to varying dimensions. If you need to order additional material to finish the job, the new fabric may come from a different dye lot and not match.

The safest way to estimate is to make a layout of each section to scale. To do this you will need a 16- to 25-inch metal tape measure, a scale rule, a pencil, and graph paper. When measuring for large sofas or chairs, you may need to use three or four sheets of graph paper taped together lengthwise. First, select your working scale, 1" = 1' works best). Next, draw two vertical lines down the length of the page showing the scaled-down width of the intended fabric (usually 54 inches wide). All the parts of the chair or sofa have to fit within this fabric width. Using the same process as used with dress patterns, the upholsterer will gently take apart the old fabric pieces and use them as patterns to cut out the new fabric.

Make a parts list and measure each part to be upholstered. For example: chair back: 24w x 18h; chair seat: 24w x 32d, and so forth. The parts list for an armchair, for example, would include inside back (patterns need to be centered here first), inside arms (you will need two arm measurements), cushion top, cushion bottom, cushion boxing, decking, skirt front, skirt back, two skirt sides, four inside skirt pleats, front border, two outside arms, outside back, length of welting, and any decorative trim. Next, using the scale rule, draw each section to scale on the graph paper between the lines marking the fabric width. The final total length of fabric on the graph paper will quickly show the total yardage needed.

For every 10 yards of fabric you estimate, add an extra 40 inches length for returns, decking, seams, folding, and sewing allowances. If the upholstery is to be quilted, an additional 10 percent of fabric is required.

When using fabrics shorter than the standard 54 inches you will need additional lengths because the shorter widths will not cover as much.

If Fabric is:	Additional Fabric Required
36 inches wide	50%
45 inches wide	20%
48 inches wide	15%
50/52 inches wide	10%

When measuring for welts, add 1 1/2 inches of fabric width times whatever length of welting is required. One-half inch is needed to wrap around the welt cord with two flaps one-half inch each to sew onto the fabric. Although welting looks small on a finished piece of upholstery, it actually uses quite a bit of fabric that has to be calculated into the final yardage count. Double welting takes twice as much yardage as single welting.

The popularity of leather upholstered furniture is a mainstay in the design industry. Leather is sold by the hide and sometimes several hides are needed to cover a sofa, loveseat, etc. When using two or more hides, color matching can be critical and sending for a CFA (cutting for approval) is a most. Leather comes in different grades of softness, texture and price.

Many leathers are embossed with patterns and designs that can make a gorgeous and outstanding piece of furniture. Rich colors of burgundy, cinnamon, brick, olive, sage, and terra cotta are some of the more desirable choices. Mixing of upholstery fabrics and leather on a single piece is a new design trend. Using two tone leathers and a combination of tapestry with leather on cushions is currently very popular. Hides are sold in square-foot increments, therefore, to estimate for leather upholstery, convert yardage to square feet by multiplying by 18 (18 square feet equals 1 yard of 54-inch fabric).

Pattern Repeats. Pattern repeats must be centered on the inside back, outside back, arms, and seat cushions. Because pattern repeats over 24 inches wide are difficult to fit on seat cushions, extra yardage is always needed for these wide repeats.

If Repeat is:	Additional Fabric Required
3 to 14 inches	10%
15 to 19 inches	15%
20 to 27 inches	20%
28 to 36 inches	25%
Over 36 inches	35%

For example, when the fabric is narrow, such as 48 inches, and there is a pattern repeat of 24 inches, an additional 35 percent of fabric is needed to complete the upholstery. (See both charts and add together the percentages.)
The fabric is 48 inches wide, which requires 20 percent more fabric. The repeat is 18 inches wide, which requires 15 percent more fabric. A total of 35 percent extra fabric is needed.

Upholstered Walls. Upholstering walls is an effective and decorative way to cover damaged and cracked plaster walls in older homes. Padded walls also act as sound insulation from outside noise as well as from noise from adjoining rooms. Upholstered walls also help to insulate the interior.

Patterned or striped fabrics hide seams, but they also are a challenge for pattern matching. To upholster walls, first cover the walls with quilt batting in a single thickness. Then sew and staple the decorative fabric in place at the ceiling, floor, and around doors and windows. Cover the staples with glued-on gimp or decorative braid. Measure for yardage by the strip method or by linear feet. (See Chapter Two, Wallcoverings, page 36.)

Various Sofa Styles

Tight back, box seat cushions, rolled arm with insert panels, shirred skirt

Pillow back cushions, extra decorative pillows, rolled arm with insert panels, rolled seat cushions, banded base and upholstered legs

Loose pillow back, rolled and pleated arm, bench "T" seat cushion, tailored skirt

Knife-edge cushions with welt trim, box arms, solid base, upholstered legs

Box seat and back cushions, rolled arm, tailored skirt

Box seat and back cushions with welt trim, wood arms, banded base

Pillow back, box seat cushions with welt trim, double banded base and arm insert panels

Arm Styles	**Skirt Styles**	**Base Styles**

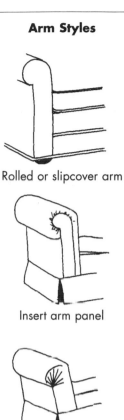

Rolled or slipcover arm

Tailored skirt

Banded base

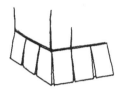

Box pleated skirt

Recessed platform base

Insert arm panel

Fan pleated arm

Tailored skirt with pleated corners

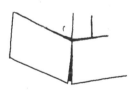

Upholstered leg base

Box arm

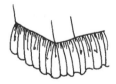

Shirred or gathered skirt

Skirted base

Tailoredskirt with gathered corners

Shirred base

Various Chair Styles

Club chair with
knife-edge cushions

Slipper chair
with box cushions
and shirred base

Club chair with box seat
cushion, loose pillow back
and arm inserts

Occassional chair with
welt trim, arm inserts, box
seat cushion, T back
cushion, pleated skirt

Occasional chair with fan
pleated arms, T seat
cushion, pillow back, welt
trim, corner gathered skirt

Occasional chair with box
seat & back cushions,
rolled arms,
pleated corner skirt

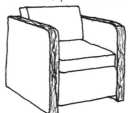

Club chair with
box seat & back cushions,
and wooden arms

Club chair with rolled &
tufted back, rolled seat
cushion, arm inserts with
welt trim and banded base

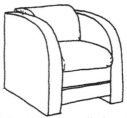

Club chair with rolled seat
& back cushions, waterfall
arms and banded base

Executive desk chair with
tufted back and tight seat

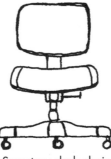

Secretary desk chair

Decorative period chair

Ottoman Styles

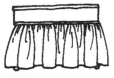

Box cushion with
welt trim and
gathered skirt

Tufted cushion,
banded base
with wood legs

Banded box
cushion with
fringe skirt

Box cushion,
banded base,
casters

Tufted cushion,
tailored and
pleated skirt

Box cushion,
tailored skirt

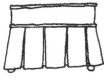

Box cushion with
welt trim and
pleated skirt

Silk sofa with washed chenille pillows trimmed with fringe.

Yardage Chart. This yardage chart was compiled to give a broad example of upholstery dimensions and corresponding yardages. This chart will work for your most commonly used upholstery pieces, however, the safest way is to always measure and diagram.

YARDAGE CHART		
Style	Size	Yardage 54″ Plain
Ottoman	20 x 24	3½
	20 x 26	3½
	26 x 26	3½
	24 x 30	3¾
Bench	36	3½
	48	4½
	60	5
Chaise	70	11½
	78	12½
	88	14½
Chair		
Armless	26 x 36	6½
Barrel	33 x 36½	6½
Loose back and seat cushion	20 x 26	8
Tight back, T-cushion	35½ x 36	8¼
Channel back, square cushion	34 x 34	7½
Tub	28 x 28	5
T-cushions back and seat	31½ x 36	8½
Wing	31w x 34d x 47h	6½
Wing	31w x 34d x 42h	7½
Love Seat		
Loose cushions	66	16¾
Tight back, 2 pillows	68	15¼
Bench cushion, 5 pillows	71	16
T-cushions, 7 pillows	72	15
Sofas		
Tight back, T-cushion	76	14¼
Bench seat, 5 pillows	80	17
T-cushions back and seat	84	17
Loose cushions	86	17½
Loose cushions, skirt	92	17½
Tight back, Loose seat cushion, skirt	96	18
Loose seat & back cushion, skirt	101	21

COST ESTIMATING

When estimating for any upholstered piece, you will need to factor in two costs: the fabric and trim cost, and the labor cost. If the upholsterer is building a custom piece from the frame up, there will be additional material costs. When an imported Italian wood frame is used with exposed hand carving, such as an imported Italian dining chair, then the material costs are higher than using a less expensive frame. There are many chair companies that import all types of upholstery frames. You can order them and have them shipped directly to the upholstery shop for covering.

TIME ESTIMATING

The time needed for an upholsterer to custom-build or to reupholster a piece of furniture can range anywhere from one week to six weeks after all fabrics have been received. This will depend on the quantity and sizes of the pieces to be upholstered, the amount of detail work, the expertise of the upholsterer and the number of workers within the upholstery shop. In large shops, there could be three or four laborers working on one piece of upholstery. For example, one worker would remove the old fabric, stuffing, springs, and webbing from the piece; another worker would repair the frame by renailing, redoweling corners, retying coil springs, and repairing any scratches or nicks to exposed wood; and still another worker would cut, sew, and reupholster the piece. When it is a one-person operation the work goes more slowly.

CHOOSING AN UPHOLSTERY WORKROOM

Upholstery workrooms are the most difficult workrooms to select because there are many degrees of competency even among those who have been in the business for a long time. The type of upholstery required for a specific job will determine your choice of upholsterer. There are individual upholsterers who have a small shop or work out of their garage. They take in a limited amount of work each month. If you choose one of these shops, you might have trouble getting large projects finished on a timely basis. Smaller workrooms can be utilized for smaller jobs or even for the overflow from bigger jobs given to larger upholstery shops. The main business of some of these upholstery shops comes from automobile and boat reupholsteries, which can be extremely different from working with delicate silks and fine tapestries.

The best upholsterers are found by referrals from other professional designers. Looking in the Yellow Pages and visiting several shops to inspect and evaluate their work is another way to find an upholsterer. Talk to the owner to find out how he or she qualifies the staff. Are they detail-oriented? Do they work with fine fabrics? Will they deliver on time? Ask for a price list and a list of client references from each shop you visit. When you call the references, ask if you can see the finished work.

Many highly qualified upholstery shops have an owner who supervises, plus two to six other upholsterers who specialize in expensive fabrics or leathers, or custom construction of frames, springs, and finishes of exposed woods. These shops can take on a whole houseful of furniture to reupholster or make custom-curved sofas, chairs, banquettes for restaurants, upholstered walls, and so forth. Shops like these are often quite expensive, so get them to explain in detail why and how they charge. Their explanations may give you an insight into their working philosophy. Custom-made upholstery is an art demanding the most skilled upholstery craftspeople. They should be perfectionists who take special care with details to create beautiful upholstered furniture.

EXAMPLE OF FINAL CUSTOM UPHOLSTERY COSTS

The Garthwaits are a couple with two school-age children. They have decided to reupholster the sofa and two chairs in their family room. The sofa is 96 inches long and has a tight back, a loose seat cushion, and a skirt. The Garthwaits selected a textured fabric 54 inches wide. They also want arm covers and would like a fabric protector sprayed onto the finished sofa.

Their two chairs have T-cushions both for the back and the seat. The fabric they have selected is plain, textured, and 54 inches wide. They also want arm covers for the chairs and would like them to be sprayed with a fabric protector.

Sofa and Chair Measurements
Sofa: 96" long
2 Chairs: 31½" width x 36" height

According to the yardage chart on page 170, a 96" sofa would require 18 yards of fabric, and two 31½" x 36" T-cushion chairs would require 8½ yards of fabric each, for a total of 17 yards for both chairs.

After you have completed measuring, calculating, and estimating, present the final figures to the client on a contract. The final figures would look something like this:

Sofa
Fabric: Pattern—Lavar; color—Gindo; 19 yards
(one extra yard for arm covers) @ $75.00 * = $1,425.00
Guardian Fabric Protection; 19 yards @5.00=   95.00
Labor: Sofa–18 yards @35.00 =   630.00
Pair of arm covers @ 30.00 =   30.00

2 Lounge Chairs
Fabric: Pattern—Emir; color—Taupe; 18 yards
(one extra yard for arm covers) @ $72.00 = $1,296.00
Guardian Fabric Protection; 18 yards   @ 5.00 =   90.00
Labor: 2 chairs–18 yards @ 35.00 =   630.00
2 pair arm covers@ 30.00 =   60.00

Subtotal	$4, 256.00
Tax 7,5% **	319.20
TOTAL	$4,575.20

Estimated time for fabrication: two to three weeks after receipt of all fabrics.

* All figures are based on 2001 Arizona prices.
** Each state would calculate tax differently according to their state laws. Some states apply tax on newly manufactured products only. Check your state laws to see what sale and use taxes apply.

Upholstery Work Order

Date: _____

P.O. # _____

Designer: _____

Address: _____

Phone: _____

Address: _____

Phone: _____

Upholstery
Workroom: _____

Address: _____

Phone: _____

Style	Fabric	Yards	Color	Pattern Repeat	Arm Style	Skirt Style	Base Style	Cushion Style	Cushion Filling	Seat Specs	Back Specs	Contrast Welts or Trims	Fabric Protection Applied	Arm Covers
1.														
2.														
3.														
4.														
5.														
6.														

Special instructions and diagrams:

Upholstery Work Order

Date: June 5, 2001

P.O. #: 1690

Designer: Carol Sampson

Address: 8705 Camelback View
Scottsdale, AZ

Phone: (480) 956-5656

Address: Mrs. Arriver
14275 North Vista
Scottsdale, AZ

Phone: (480) 683-4567

Upholstery Workroom: Cranmor's Upholstery

Address: 3050 1st Ave.
Tempe, AZ

Phone: (480) 755-1234

Style	Fabric	Yards	Color	Pattern Repeat	Arm Style	Skirt Style	Base Style	Cushion Style	Cushion Filling	Seat Specs	Back Specs	Contrast Welts or Trims	Fabric Protection Applied	Arm Covers
1. #405 sofa	P+P lara	19	Ginko	6"	rolled/Tailored	Tailored	Solid	Removable	Dacron w/Down	Box	Tight	0	yes	1 pair
2. #810 2-chairs Swivel	P+P	18	Taupe	0	Fan pleated	Tight	Brushed	Removable	Dacron w/Down	Box	Foam	0	yes	2 pair
3.														
4.														
5.														
6.														

Special instructions and diagrams:

① Check frame for any loose corners + replace or reinforce.

② Check cushions for any breakdown + replace if necessary.

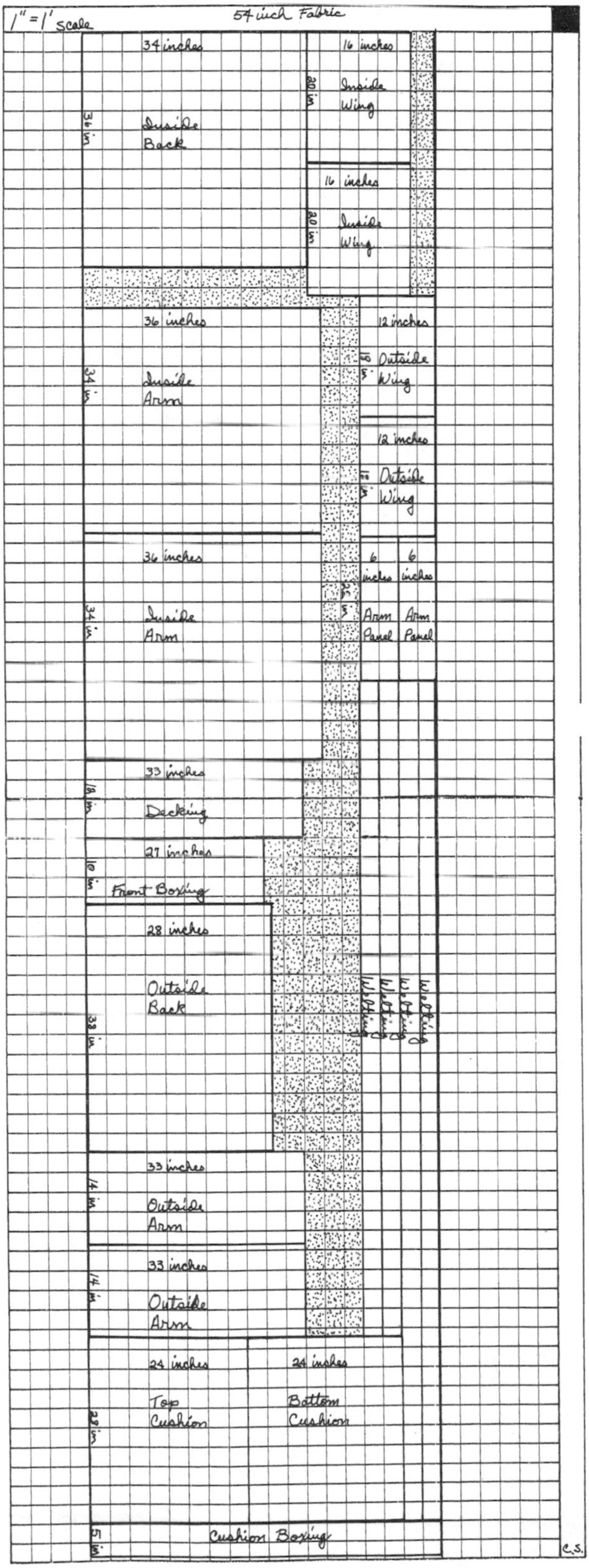

54 inch Fabric

34 inches

16 inches

20 in.

Inside
Wing

34 in.

Inside
Back

16 inches

20 in.

Inside
Wing

36 inches

12 inches

34 in.

Inside
Arm

10 in.

Outside
Wing

12 inches

11 in.

Outside
Wing

36 inches

6
inches

6
inches

34 in.

Inside
Arm

5 in.

Arm
Panel

Arm
Panel

33 inches

18 in.

Decking

27 inches

10 in.

Front Boxing

28 inches

Outside
Back

33 in.

33 inches

14 in.

Outside
Arm

33 inches

14 in.

Outside
Arm

24 inches

24 inches

Top
Cushion

Bottom
Cushion

28 in.

5 in.

Cushion Boxing

C.S.

Chapter Eight

HARD FLOOR COVERINGS

Canterra stone entry with a black slate border and limestone beige square inserts.

Interior flooring has evolved over thousands of years from its beginning as primitive, beaten clay. These early floors were unadorned, unpainted, and dusty, and had to be scoured or sanded to keep them semi-clean. Eventually, brick and tile became more common indoor floor coverings. The evolution eventually progressed to beautiful, elegant wood, marble, limestone, sandstone, and slate floor coverings, and today we are able to choose from a wealth of durable products in a wide range of styles and prices.

Brick. Brick is one of the oldest, most widely used building materials. Brick is a basic component of buildings and countless other structures all over the world. Historically, brick ovens became the best means of cooking certain foods, and the radiating warmth from these ovens also helped heat rooms.

Brick is made by placing clay—a common, easy-to-find material in many geographical locations—in a form or mold and drying it in the sun or in a very hot kiln until it is solid and hard. When the use of bricks for building became commonplace, their appearance became more varied; bricks were designed in different sizes, shapes and colors. Depending on the source and kind of clay, bricks can range in color from white, pale yellow, and pink to orange, red, brown, and even purple. The term "red brick" refers to the colored clay early settlers of the east coast of America used extensively to make the red brick buildings now typical of that part of the country.

Colorful, glazed brickwork was used in the ancient cities of the Babylonian-Assyrian empire, and the architecture of the ancient Egyptians also relied extensively on brick. Walls were built using sun-dried bricks covered with plaster, asphalt, or slabs of stone and topped with decorative mosaic work made from glazed pieces of brick. An example of this highly developed, artistic workmanship can be seen in the Ishtar Gate (a remnant of one of the eight original gates to the ancient, wall-surrounded city of Babylon; the Ishtar Gate was on the northern side of the city). A sculpted, enameled brick bull is framed in black and terra-cotta bricks and bas-relief Babylonian lions are beautifully detailed in rectangular, glazed bricks—some white with gold manes, some gold with green manes—on a light-blue background with a border of daisies overhead.

The floors of most medieval castles were covered with bricks. A fine example from 1340 A.D. is preserved at the Baron's Hall, Penshurst Place, England. The worn brick floor uses what appear to be two colors of terra-cotta brick as well as black brick, with an octagonal outline in the center where logs were burned to heat the hall.

Some of the best examples of ancient brickwork can be seen in Byzantine churches (dating from 330 A.D. to 1450 A.D.). Byzantine artisans and builders laid the brick in herringbone patterns or set it diagonally across floors and up walls. They also used brickwork trim in the borders, frames and bands running around the walls and floors of the churches.

During the Renaissance, Italian builders adopted brick herringbone patterns for residences, gardens and country churches. Brickwork dating from ancient times down to the twenty-first century can be seen all over Europe. The adobe bricks commonly associated with Native American building traditions in the American Southwest have, in fact, also been used in many other warm, dry locales for centuries.

Bricks are durable, weather-resistant, fireproof, easy to maintain, and appropriate for interiors and exteriors. They can be made by machine or by hand. Face bricks, or common bricks, have straight, sharp edges and are uniform in color and texture. Because they are so weather resistant, these bricks are the most suitable for exterior, exposed walls or sides of buildings. Paving or floor bricks are fired at extreme temperatures to harden them; this increases their resistance to abrasion and compression and reduces their capacity to absorb moisture. Previously-used brick is a valuable product to recycle from older buildings because of its beautiful, weathered character and color. Brick flooring weighs less than stone flooring and needs less underlying structural support.

Concrete. The Romans made the use of masonry material similar to modern concrete standard. They found this completely new building material strong, inexpensive, and adaptable for building roads, constructing columns, flooring, walls, and decorative details. They used concrete as a substructure and covered it with finer finish materials such as marble, alabaster, brick, or stucco.

Concrete is made from a wet mixture of gravel or small stones, sand, lime and water. The mixture is poured into preconstructed wooden forms and left to dry or cure for several days or weeks. Today it is widely used commercially for buildings, roadways, barrier walls, dams, bridges, stairways, and hundreds of other structures. It is used to make the foundation for most residential homes, and to make patios in gardens, pottery, for decorative elements such as columns, statuary, fountains, and outside tables and benches. Today, as in the ancient past, concrete is also used as the substructure for surfacing materials such as marble, granite, brick, rock, and stucco.

Exposed concrete flooring is an inexpensive way to solve a budget problem for an interior in a commercial building or a residence. Rather than leave the concrete floor flat and smooth, there are two ways to give it character. It can be scored while still wet with designs in bold forms or geometric patterns of diamonds, squares, rectangles and lines. Or, the surface of solid concrete can be sandblasted to create a pattern, texture, border, or logo. After the dust and dirt are cleaned away, it can then be stained, waxed, or painted in several colors to match or set the decor. Usually, several layers of colors are used to give unusual texturing and contrasting to the design. Finally, a protective coating or sealer is applied to protect it from foot traffic and abrasion from furniture.

Another innovation in concrete has been the use of colored tile sizes in both muted and vivid palettes. The new, full range of sizes and shapes offers exciting opportunities for creating concrete floors in the same manner in which ceramic tile floors or stone floors are designed. Most new tiles have to be custom-ordered from concrete fabricators, and they must still be properly sealed to prevent wear and traffic patterns.

A square foot or a custom price is used to estimate the cost to design in concrete. The cost depends on the amount of layers used for the design and whether the concrete will be designed at the wet stage or sandblasted onto existing concrete flooring.

Stone. Stone, whether it is granite, marble, limestone, travertine, or sandstone, has been used extensively throughout history in every country and culture. Ancient peoples carved a variety of stone and left us a record of their communities, daily lives, and religious symbols. They quarried stone locally or imported it along trade routes all over the world. They cut, carved, and decorated all types of stone for temples, churches, basilicas, and residences and adorned walls with stone murals, borders, cornices, frieze and bas-relief designs. They combined different colors of marble, granite, and limestone to create gorgeous floors, columns, tables, and chairs that are still marvels thousands of years later.

Granite and limestone slabs covered floors, and granite columns supported the interior walls and heavy roofs of ancient Egyptian temples dating from 3000 B.C. Many colorful granite pillars or columns dating back to 1500 B.C. have been found in Egypt.

Stone mosaic work reached specialized levels in Greece, Rome and Pompeii, and India. Many beautiful ancient Greek temples were built using polished and painted sandstone in a colorful array of blues, yellow and green foils, outlines in vermilion and more foils in red and blue. Alabaster was often used in Assyrian reliefs and murals, intricately decorated with stylized leaves and trees. Limestone columns in India dating from the reign of King Asako in the third century B.C. are completely carved and layered with rows of ornamentation believed to be copied from textile and carpet patterns.

Today, builders in the United States commonly use shell stone from the Southeast, canterra from the Southwest and a man-made stone, agglomerate marble, better known as terrazzo.

There are three categories of natural stone: igneous, sedimentary and metamorphic. Each is formed by its environment and has its own unique properties such as color range, texture, shading, pitting and durability.

Igneous rock is the hardest of the three kinds, formed by solidification of molten magma under tremendous heat and pressure below the earth's surface. Granite is an igneous stone, and is the densest of that group. It consists of quartz and feldspars—a group of crystalline rock materials. The combinations and quantities of minerals in molten magma create granite's huge variety of colors and hues. It ranges from white, cream, gold, pink, rust, brown, beige, green, and blue to black-and-white, black-and-brown, and black-and-blue. Granite has a hard, dense sur-

Flooring is irregular sandstone with slate squares and black granite accents.

face and a granular texture and can stand up to oil, alcohol and chemical cleaners that stain other stones. Granite is a beautiful, natural material suitable for countertops, showers, tub surrounds, walls, flooring or just about anywhere. Granite is top-of-the-line expensive—estimated and sold by the linear foot for countertops and by the square foot if it is used for flooring in a square tile size. It's available in custom slabs or tile squares in sizes ranging from 4 x 4, 8 x 8, 12 x 12, 13 x 13, 16 x 16 and 24 x 24 inches. Granite is usually polished and protected with a sealant.

Sedimentary stone is softer than igneous, and is formed by deposits of sediment over thousands of years. There are five kinds of sedimentary stone: limestone, travertine, sandstone, shell stone, and canterra stone.

Limestone is formed from pulverized and compressed shells and inorganic remains of organisms. Colors are usually neutral and range from dusty grays, and soft beiges to pale golds and creamy whites. Limestone is suitable for countertops, showers, fireplace-facing, entryways, and floors because it is water resistant, heatproof, and very durable. Limestone is more porous than granite or marble and requires a sealant and regular maintenance to protect it from oil, alcohol, acids in cleaning products, and the chemicals present in some water supplies that can stain its finish.

Travertine is a type of limestone. It is a massive, sometimes layered, calcium carbonate formed from spring (especially hot springs) water deposition. It has natural pits and air pockets, which should be filled with grout and polished smooth before being used for flooring. Colors range from soft pinks, tans, and grays to dramatic dark browns, greens, and blacks. Since travertine is a derivative of limestone, it too needs to be sealed against stains.

Sandstone or shale is formed from mineral and rock fragments transported from their original source through erosion and deposited elsewhere by water. Sandstone is usually pale beige, pink and tan. Sandstone is great for flooring and should be sealed for indoor use to protect it from stains. It is generally sold as flagstone, which is sandstone split into flat pieces.

Shell stone is a sedimentary stone found primarily in Florida and Central America composed of small, crushed pieces of shells and fossils. It usually has a shell-like texture, and is white with fragments of peach, pink and gray. It is porous, and requires regular sealing to protect it from stains. Shell stone is most commonly used for walls and flooring and is sold in 12 x 12 inch and 24 x 24 inch tile squares.

Canterra stone is found in sedimentary deposits along riverbeds in certain regions of Mexico. It comes in five neutral colors and is primarily used in the southwest United States for columns, moldings, and paving tiles. Because canterra is porous, it needs sealant to protect it from stains.

There are three types of metamorphic stone: marble, slate and quartzite. Metamorphic rocks are also sedimentary but have gone through a pronounced change effected by pressure, heat, and water that results in their compact, highly crystalline condition.

Some of Europe's most beautiful architecture was built with marble. Greek temples were embellished with sculptured marble and marble wall tiles; the support columns of the roof of the Caryatides Portico, for example, are marble sculptures of women. The Palace of Versailles and Chateau Fontainebleau in France are famed for their many-colored, intricately patterned marble walls, floors, and stairs.

In Italy, elaborate marble checkerboards, scrolls, medallions, and borders in every color combination adorn palaces. Indeed, much of the world's most beautiful marble comes from Italy, where it has been popular since the Renaissance.

The beauty of marble comes from the veins, streaks and washes of color caused by minerals that meander through the porous carbonate rock. Marble's porous structure also means that it will stain easily unless its surface is protected by sealant on a regular basis. It is not suitable for countertops because oil, alcohol or chemicals can permanently stain the surface, but makes durable floors and walls. Polished marble can be slippery when wet and caution should be exercised before installing it in shower or tub areas.

Small, unpolished marble tiles can be aged to give them an old-world appearance. These tiles are tumbled in a solution of water, sand, and mild acid in large barrels. The result is antique, weathered, European. Marble tiles and slabs are sold in various sizes, shapes, and styles allowing for flexibility in design and pattern. Once considered a luxury, marble is now being more widely used, for purposes throughout homes. Large marble slabs and tiles of 24 x 24 inches down to smaller accent pieces called buttons or inlaid squares are being used in bathrooms, kitchens and on floors.

Borders of marble, intricately designed medallions, marble mosaics and other insert pieces are enjoying new popularity because of several new manufacturing processes. These designs are pre-mounted on a net backing to keep the many small pieces in a fixed position until the installer places the pattern in the desired location. This cuts down on the intensive labor normally required to put such custom designs together on site. Many medallions and insert pieces are sold individually. Most decorative border pieces come in 4 x 12 or 6 x 12 inch pieces and are sold by the linear foot.

The use of diamond-saw techniques for cutting marble make it more competitive in price with quality ceramic tile products. Also, new sealers help protect the surfaces of porous stones, especially marble. Patterns, logos, and pictures can be "inlaid" directly into marble with laser-jets, thus allowing endless creative possibilities. Chemical treatments, using muriatic acid solution, can etch designs into the marble or give it a textured pattern or design.

Slate is another dense, fine-grained metamorphic rock produced by the compression of various sedimentary materials such as clay or shale and tends to split along natural fissures or grains, giving it an uneven surface. It can be polished or honed to smooth out its irregularities. It's colors are usually dark, ranging from grays, purples, and blues to charcoal, beige, brown, and black. Slate also needs sealer and maintenance.

Quartzite is a hardened granular rock with a pebbly surface. It makes very durable, hard flooring material. Its colors are brown to black.

Terrazzo is a manufactured, or agglomerate, stone created by embedding chips of marble, quartz, or granite into mortar or concrete and then polishing the surface. Used extensively in the fifties and sixties as a flooring surface, especially in the South, it is undergoing a revival and is now being used in tile sizes with more colors. It can have poor color retention and lacks the toughness of real stone, but new versions are constantly being improved.

Laminate. Laminate flooring is a relatively new product manufactured by several domestic companies: Bruce, Formica, Wilsonart and one international company, Prego. Laminate flooring simulates hardwood, stone or ceramic tile.

Laminate flooring is a multilayer composite of materials designed to be strong, easy to maintain, stain-proof, water resistant and much less expensive than real wood or stone. The layers are laminated under intense heat and pressure. Each company's product varies slightly, but they all have a common construction of between five to seven layers.

The top is a wear layer of polyurethane, acrylic or a combination of the two to seal and protect the surface from scuffs, dents, stains, wear, fading, burns and foot traffic patterns. The design layer is next, this can simulate various wood colors and grains, or it can imitate many ceramic tile patterns, or it can replicate the textures and colors of stones such as marble, slate, terrazzo, etc. The third layer is the

Floors are porcelain tile with black granite inserts. Counter has slate and glass tiles. Walls are raked plaster with a faux finish.

core—high density, water-resistant fiberboard put together in a tongue and groove construction for easy installation. Several companies use kraft papers or a melamine back layer underneath the core to lock out moisture. The last layer smooths out imperfections in the existing floor that may cause warping and buckling.

All of the laminate flooring companies offer a fifteen to sixteen year warranty. Some laminate products are better suited to regions of the country with large amounts of rain and snow because of their extra moisture barrier. When selecting these products, read about the special features from each company that might determine which is the better choice for the job.

Each company has detail and accessory products to complete the installation beautifully. These extra products are sold individually, such as moldings that include quarter rounds, baseboards, stair nosing and end caps. There are also transition pieces that include T-moldings used in doorways or thresholds to join or bridge two areas of laminate flooring. And, there are reducers or transition strips used in doorways to join laminate flooring and carpet.

Laminate floor systems are popular because they are durable and affordable. Prices and durabilty vary, but are comparable to those of carpet, which in general lasts ten to fifteen years. For added protection, use felt protectors on furniture legs and replace plastic casters with rubber ones. Laminate flooring is measured and sold by the square foot.

Vinyl. Vinyl or resilient flooring is made of printed or embossed manufactured solid or blended materials resembling the texture of stone, wood or ceramic tile. A wide selection of traditional or contemporary patterns is available in many designs and colors. Vinyl floors have a protective surface-layer either of acrylic or silicon for easy maintenance and stain resistance. Most resilient floors require little more than damp mopping to keep their surfaces looking great.

Vinyl flooring has a wide range of styles, prices and warranties. It can be used inexpensively for residential locations, but there are also luxury vinyls for use in upper-end shops, restaurants, museums and malls.

Vinyls can be purchased in twelve foot sheets or in twelve foot squares in thin, 10 mm thick layers. There are three different grades of vinyl flooring. The least expensive vinyl combines vinyl resins with filler. The middle-priced vinyl is a rotovinyl—a printed pattern sealed with a top coat. The most expensive is an inlaid vinyl with vinyl granules fused together on a solid pattern that goes all the way through to the backing; this is also the most durable of the residential vinyls.

Two to four page limited warranties accompany the residential vinyls, but will not always cover dents, cuts, gouges, burns, scuffs, scratches, stains, fading or discoloration from heat or sunlight. These limited warranties are generally good for two to five years to the original owner only.

Upper end, luxury vinyls are used in the international market and are much thicker (25 mm), designed to withstand heavy traffic in public areas. This luxury vinyl has endless custom-design possibilities, from standard shapes and sizes to wildly creative patterns, borders, logos, and medallions. Curves, circles and special patterns can be perfectly designed into any nonstandard pattern using a computer-generated floor plan as a cutting guide to ensure accuracy. These vinyls are very expensive and require an experienced subcontractor to install them. Their price is usually based on the size, design and intricacy of the installation.

The warranties for luxury vinyls are much more comprehensive and offer a limited ten year protection against wearing out under the normal rigors of a busy commercial environment, anywhere in the world.

Tile. Ceramic tile is one of the world's oldest decorative treatments for floors and walls. The Egyptians used tiles for wall and architectural decoration. An especially popular rich blue color was obtained from copper and required great skill and patience to create. The Assyrians used colored tiles to decorate friezes showing archers and animals in relief.

The interiors of many palaces of the late Islamic period were built and decorated with complicated tile mosaics. The Alhambra (1309–1354 A.D.) in Granada, Spain is an excellent example; its walls and floors are embellished with glazed tile in subdued tones. Many Moorish buildings in Spain have tile dados or wainscot that extend up the walls three or four feet and were bordered by a band with a repeating pattern. Tiles were used everywhere on door and window facings, window jambs and seats, risers of steps, linings of niches and arches, in fountains, washbasins, pools and floors. Mosaics were a popular and beautiful form of mural

Bank lobby has plank wood borders and square slate insets.

decorations used extensively in early Christian and Byzantine churches as well.

In 1455 A.D., tile from Spain was first admitted into Venice, and the Italians took off with it. Today, Italy manufactures 40% of the world's supply of tile. Tile is also produced in other European countries and in North and South America, but it often strongly resembles Italian tile.

Tile is available in infinite combinations of size, shape, color, pattern, and texture. Tile floors are durable, easy to clean, won't stain or fade, and are color-fast, abrasion resistant, waterproof and beautiful. There are several types of tile, including the following: mosaic, unglazed, quarried, porcelain, and decorative in glazed or glass styles.

Tile is made of clay either air-dried naturally or dried at high temperature in a kiln. When kiln-dried, it is in a "bisque" or unglazed state.

Quarry tiles are unglazed and come in the natural clay colors of yellow, rust, brown, and terra-cotta. Unglazed tiles are less slippery than glazed ones, and are therefore suitable for both indoor and outdoor use. Typical sizes are 6 x 6, 8 x 8, and 12 x 12 inch squares and 3 x 6 and 4 x 8 inch rectangles. Though very durable, they benefit from sealer to protect against stains in high traffic areas.

Another unglazed tile is terra-cotta, which means "cooked earth" in Italian. Terra-cotta tiles have been used in many places all over Europe but are especially recognized as a Southwestern American tile. Saltillo tiles (named for the area in

Mexico where they are produced) are made by putting local clay into wooden forms, which are left in the sun to dry and then fired at a low temperature. Their colors vary, with shadings blending from dark to light on the same tile. Sometimes animal tracks add to their rustic effect. These tiles are very porous and aren't always appropriate for use outdoors in freezing climates. Terra-cotta tiles, whether used indoors or outdoors, need sealer to prevent stains. They come in octagonal and 12 x 12 inch sizes with some irregular edges and widths that contribute to their rustic quality.

When tile is glazed, the bisque tile is given a facial coating of color and then fired, creating a smooth, impermeable surface. Some nonslip floor tiles also have textured or matte finish glazes, and some glazes have abrasives added for better traction. Like marble, glazed tile is unwise in wet areas because it is slippery. Glazed floor tiles will usually hold up to heavy traffic, stains and fading.

The Porcelain Enamel Institute (PEI) uses the following systerm to rate glazed tile's resistance to wear.

Group 1   Light residential traffic suitable for bathrooms, bedrooms and vertical surfaces.

Group 2   Moderate residential traffic suitable for all residential areas EXCEPT kitchens, entry halls and areas subject to outdoor traffic.

Group 3   High residential traffic suitable for all residential and some light commercial areas.

Group 4   Commercial traffic suitable for hotels lobbies, restaurants and banks.

Porcelain tiles, or payers, are dense, nonporous bisques made from highly refined clay fired at 2000 degrees Fahrenheit to form an impervious or vitreous body. Porcelain tiles are waterproof and stain-resistant, and thus ideal for countertops, floors, swimming pools and high traffic areas. They can be given a textured or matt finish to make them slip-resistant. Porcelain tiles can have the look of slate, limestone, marble or quarry tiles without their disadvantages. They come in 12 x 12 inch squares and 4x6 inch rectangles.

Mosaic tiles are very small (one to two inch) squares of colored stone or glass set in cement and arranged in a picture or pattern. They are made in an infinite variety of colors and shapes, from squares, rectangles, octagons, and hexagons to custom shapes and sizes. Mosaics are either commercially produced or handmade, one-of-a-kind, free-form artworks. The commercially made mosaics are mounted onto a net backing in large sections, such as a 12 x 12 inch sheet, ready to align to the pattern or design, pressed into the adhesive and grouted when dry. Using sheet-mounted mosaics is not as labor intensive as placing individual small pieces into a piece of artwork that fits together like a puzzle. Art mosaics have to be laid out in a factory or art studio, mounted on backing sections, moved to the job site, installed and grouted. Or they are laid out at the job site. Either way, art mosaics are always much more expensive.

Mosaics are made of clay and can be glazed or unglazed. Their small size coupled with the multiple grout joints make mosaics excellent choices for areas frequently exposed to water, such as bathroom floors, showers, countertops, pool decks, and outdoor areas. Many manufactured mosaics have scratch-resistant glazes. Unglazed, tumbled or honed mosaics can be used for countertops and floors but a sealer is always a safe addition to protect against stains.

Glass tiles have been around for centuries; Moreno glass was developed in Venice in the seventh century. Small glazed and glass mosaics with gold and silver leaf and a huge array of other beautiful colors elaborately decorate the interior and exterior of St. Mark's Basilica.

In today's market, there is an incredible selection of glass tile available. There are transparent glass tiles in multiple, smoked colors, and opaque and shimmering iridescent glazes. Other glass tiles are hand painted in primary colors or soft tones, and can be used to create unique custom murals or theme tiles set as accents on a large, solid tile background. Some glass tiles have raised relief subjects or running designs useful for borders. Glass tiles are naturally waterproof, making them good choices for showers, tub surrounds, backsplashes, pools, and outside fountains.

There are special grouts and adhesives available for these special glass tiles. Glass tiles are installed in the same manner as ceramic tiles, making it easy to combine them if desired.

To figure the amount of tile needed to cover an area, calculate the approximate square footage by multiplying its length by its width and add a safety amount of 5 per cent extra. Most trim pieces are sold individually or by the linear foot and are designed to finish off the open ends, edges, and corners of a tile installation. These extra pieces could include inside or outside corners, bullnose, down-angle (two rounded edges), borders, end pieces, cove, quarter round, half-round, V-cap or a radius trim.

Wood. Wood floors have graced the interiors of homes for centuries. Thick plank flooring of oak and walnut was traditional in homes in Europe and America.

After 1600 A.D., the use of elaborate herringbone and parquetry patterns in rarer woods came into vogue among the wealthy in Europe. The inlaid parquetry floors of many Tuscan villas are notable for their richness of design and elegance.

Early American colonists preferred 'Heart Pine because of its majestic size—an entire house could be built from the heartwood of one tree. These magnificent trees were impervious to rot and insects, but were overharvested and wiped out by the end of the 19th century. Today, this enduring wood is being reclaimed and recycled for new use whenever an outmoded factory or textile mill is taken down. Hardwood flooring for many colonial homes, churches, schools, and courthouses has stood the test of time and still reflects warmth, beauty and durability centuries later.

Today, wood flooring has an incredible variety of styles, finishes and colors. Wood flooring is a comfortable fit in any environment whether traditional, casual country or contemporary. Wood flooring can add warmth to a country family room, offset a contemporary living room filled with fine art, give drama to an entryway or add a rich backdrop to precious antique rugs and furnishings. Contrasting wood tones can make a border on the floor that is striking for a dining room, living room or entry.

There are several styles to work with, including wood strips in random lengths, planks, diagonals, squares, and parquet. Hardwood floor colors have a wide spectrum of tones to choose from, including bleached white, soft yellow, amber, honey, yellow-brown, chestnut, cinnamon, cherry, reddish-brown, caramel and black-brown. Each hardwood floor company has brochures with illustrations, examples, and suggestions for each style.

Hardwoods come from forests around the world and each varies in hardness. Harder woods are Hungarian oak, Canadian maple, American pecan, Malaysian merbau and Australian jarrah. The reason most gym floors are made of the hardwood maple is because it can take the severe wear and tear of running and jumping feet. Softer woods are American cherry, Scandinavian beech and birch, European ash, Swedish pine and white oak and American red oak. Pine has a beautiful look but its soft structure is not suitable flooring for kitchens, children, dogs, or activity rooms.

There are two types of hardwood flooring: solid and engineered. Top-of-the-line hardwood floors are the traditional, solid wood flooring which offers more widths, finishes, border options and surface treatments. With solid wood, you can use any type that is commercially available, especially if you're willing to pay for rarer woods such as cypress, teak, alder, or walnut. Most solid wood floors can last several hundred years when installed professionally and can be sanded down and refinished for a color change as much as three times.

The second type of hardwood floor is engineered and layered. Engineered floors are real wood layered with hardwood laminated onto several layers of plywood at 90-degree angles in a tongue-and-groove construction. This provides stability and prevents shrinkage and expansion from changes in temperature and humidity. The top surface is stained a particular color and then sealed five to six times with an advanced acrylic urethane protective finish for easy maintenance. The selection is generally limited to the woods and stains each company offers. Engineered wood floors are less expensive than solid woods and are pre-finished and easy to install.

Both kinds of wood floors are easy to maintain because of the new non-ambering acrylic finishes that prevent most of the staining and scratching that was once common with floor finishes and cleaning products of the past. Now regular vacuuming or dust mopping can get rid of the surface grit and dust which can wear out a finish. Spray wax products (Pledge, Liquid Gold and Murphy's are meant for furniture not floors) should be avoided because they leave a dangerously slick surface and cause a buildup that makes refinishing floors difficult.

Hardwood flooring is estimated by the square foot method. Multiply the length of the area to be covered by its width. Trim pieces are usually sold by the linear foot. Trim pieces include moldings and transition pieces such as quarter rounds, reducer strips (reducer strips serve as a transition between wood flooring and other flooring of different heights such as carpet, tile, etc.), stair noses, T-molds, and flush mount reducers.

COST ESTIMATING

When estimating costs for hard floor products, there will be three costs: one for the product, one for the trim products and one for the installer or subcontractor.

Material Costs. The material costs for all hard floor coverings are quoted in square feet (sq. ft.), which makes it easier to compare costs from one product to another. The material costs will always change with inflation and the popularity of certain products and new products. A rule of thumb is to measure the length times the width of an area to get the amount of square feet to be covered. Trim pieces are sold individually for tiles and stone and by the linear foot (running foot) for hardwood, laminate and vinyl.

Labor Costs. Labor costs to install hard flooring products will vary, depending on the type of product or material you are using, the amount of detail work involved and if any tear-out work is required first. The highest labor costs will be for those products that require individual cutting, such as tile, stone and solid hardwood. Less expensive labor will be charged for sheet vinyl, pre-cut laminate and pre-cut engineered hardwood floors. There will always be extra charges for detail work such as tile or stone (granite, slate, etc.) counter tops, putting together artistic patterns, inserts or dots, murals, medallions or logos. Hardwood floors that have patterns in herringbone, parquet or borders will be an extra labor charge. And, brick work will have extra charges if fancy work is requested for basket weave, herringbone or parquet designs.

Any time there is tear-out work or preparation work needed before the flooring is put down there will be extra charges. Cement floors may need repairs on cracks or nail holes before stains and finishes can be decoratively applied. The concrete floor may need to be smoothed out before new vinyl, laminate or hardwood floors are laid. Old vinyl may need to be torn up before the new tile or stone replaces it. Old carpet may need to be pulled up, hauled away and the subfloor repaired before marbles or slate can be put down correctly. Be sure to get an on-the-job quote before the labor begins so there are no surprises.

TIME ESTIMATING

The time needed to order and install hard floor covering can range anywhere from a few days to several weeks. After the installer or subcontractor has quoted the job and verified the amount of product needed, the order needs to go in. Ordering the product could take days, weeks or months depending on the type of product. Custom tile may need to be hand painted or ordered from a foreign country if it's not in stock. Granite or marble may need to be custom ordered from a different state or a foreign country to get the right color. Rare hardwoods may need to be imported from faraway places and go through customs, which is always slow. No installer will start a job until all the materials are available.

If the product is not back ordered (which would hold up the installation), the installer will schedule an installation date. Many subcontractors have several people working for them, and that will make the job go faster. If it is only a one-person operation the work goes more slowly. All of the hard floor coverings will need a two or three-step process; laying out the surfaces and then grouting or trimming and detailing the edges. Tile and stone work will require time for the layout of the materials on wet mortar and time to dry, which could take a day or so. Next, tile or stone work needs to be grouted between joints, and after that dries, it may require a sealer to be applied. If working with hardwoods, the first part of the job is to lay out the wood floor and then go back and trim out the transitions, walls or stairs. If working with cement, each stain or color added to the design will need drying time in-between coats. Vinyl may only take a day to install, depending on the size of the job and the amount of prep work needed. The least amount of time (from ordering to completion of installation) would probably be about two to three weeks.

The fall is one of the busiest times of the year for any construction or remodeling project because people want their projects done for the holidays, so don't wait until the last minute.

Selecting an installer or subcontractor. Many different installers are necessary for the various hard flooring products, and each product requires different levels of skill and expertise. Start by asking for references from other interior designers or from the supplier you went through to purchase the flooring materials. To find a qualified subcontractor or installer for tile, stone or hardwood ask for references and photos (if available). Call all references and ask questions, make notes and comments for future reference. Take into consideration pricing, reliability, quality of work and punctual performance.

Submit the same information for bid to three installers or subcontractors. Make sure they each have state licenses, workers' compensation, and insurance. If possible, check bank references and the Better Business Bureau. Give each one the same information in sketches, specifications or drawings, noting any unusual situations or scheduling times. Once bids are in and a price is worked out, plan to supervise all the work by stopping at the job site often. The relationship between you and the installer/subcontractor is crucial to a successful long-term job; make sure there is good communication and good rapport. As your professional relationship builds, trust on both sides will contribute to a rewarding, long-term connection.

EXAMPLE OF FINAL HARD FLOORING COSTS

Mr. and Mrs. Sampson have decided to add hard flooring to upgrade their home. They have hired an interior designer to help them make their choices and complete the installations. They selected porcelain tile for the floors of their master bathroom, marble tile for the front entry and hardwood flooring for their kitchen. Some tear-up work is needed for the carpet that now covers the master bathroom and entry and the old vinyl has to be pulled up in the kitchen.

Measurements

The front entry area is 6 feet by 5 feet, The kitchen is 15 feet by 13 feet and the bathroom is 14 feet by 8 feet.

Final Estimates

Entry:

6 x 5 = 30 sq. ft. Beige/White Marble squares of 12 x 12 size;

30 sq. ft. Marble @ 4.50 sq.ft. =	$ 135.00*
30 sq. ft. Labor @ 3.50 sq.ft. =	105.00
30 sq. ft. Tear-up @ .65 sq.ft. =	19.50
Subtotal =$	295.50

Kitchen:

15 x 13 = 195 sq. ft. Whitewashed, parquet wood floor;

195 sq. ft. parquet @ 5.00 sq. ft. =	975.00
195 sq. ft. Labor @ 3.00 sq. ft. =	585.00
195 sq. ft. Tear-up @ .50 sq. ft. =	97.50
Trim—quarter round—56 linear feet @ .75 linear ft. =	42.00
Subtotal =	$1,699.50

Master Bathroom:

14 x 8 = 112 sq. ft. Cream/Beige Porcelain tile in 12 x12 size:

112 sq. ft. tile @ 2.50 sq. ft. =	280.00
112 sq. ft. Labor @ 2.50 sq. ft. =	280.00
112 sq. ft. Tear-up @ .50 sq. ft. =	56.00
Subtotal =	$616.00

Tax on materials/products only:

Marble, hardwood & tile Tax 7.5%**	107.40
Entry, Kitchen, M. Bathroom Flooring	TOTAL $2,718.40

* All figures are based on 2001 Arizona prices.

** Each state would calculate tax differently according to their laws. Some states apply tax on newly manufactured products only. Check your state laws to see what sale and use taxes apply.

Hard Floor Covering

Date: May 5, 2001

P.O. # 1095

Designer: Carol Sampson

Address: 6705 Camelback Road
Scottsdale, Az

Phone: (480) 956-5656

Fax:

Installation Address:

Mr. + Mrs. Sampson
3070 Mountain
Phoenix, Az

Phone: (480) 755-6789

Fax:

Room: Front Entry   Square Feet: 30   Linear Feet: 0

Materials: Beige/Cream Marble

Labor: Tear out carpet + install marble

Trim: 0

Room: Kitchen   Square Feet: 195   Linear Feet: 56

Materials: White washed parquet floors

Labor: Tear out old vinyl floor + install wood floor

Trim: wood - quarter round

Room: Master Bedroom   Square Feet: 112   Linear Feet: 0

Materials: Porcelain tile - cream/beige

Labor: Tear out carpet + install tile floor

Trim:

Special Instructions/Drawing/Specifications:

Hard Floor Covering

Date: _____   Installation Address: _____

P.O. # _____   _____

Designer: _____   _____

Address: _____   _____

_____   Phone: _____

Phone: _____   Fax: _____

Fax: _____

Room: _____   Square Feet: _____   Linear Feet: _____

Materials _____

Labor: _____

Trim: _____

Room: _____   Square Feet: _____   Linear Feet: _____

Materials _____

Labor: _____

Trim: _____

Room: _____   Square Feet: _____   Linear Feet: _____

Materials _____

Labor: _____

Trim: _____

Special Instructions/Drawing/Specifications:

Afterword

AFTER THE ESTIMATE

Upholstered walls help insulate this office.

Estimates for each phase of the design project are presented to the client for approval. If the first estimate proves to be too high, then a revised estimate is required. Most often, the revised estimate is put together using less expensive materials since labor costs to make drapery, bed coverings, and reupholstery, usually stay the same. Estimates can also be reduced by eliminating or postponing portions of the project. Some clients have a fixed budget for a project; others are more willing and able to evaluate the design concept against the final estimates.

LETTER OF AGREEMENT

After the client approves all of the estimates for a project, the letter of agreement must be drawn up and signed by both parties before any work is begun. The letter of agreement for each project will be as individualized as your design, reflecting the custom-made aspects of the work by listing all the specifications for that particular job. Form letters of agreement can be obtained from the American Society of Interior Designers (ASID). The book *A Guide to Business Principles and Practices, Rev. Ed.* by Harry and Alan Siegel (Whitney Library of Design) is a good source for information on letters of agreement.

GOING OVER BUDGET

By working out complete estimates and discussing them thoroughly with the client before the work is begun, you can avoid running into unexpected expenses. However, unavoidable extra costs will sometimes cause the project to go over-budget. Depending on the type, you may decide to quietly absorb or split the extra expense with the client. If the expense is clearly a result of the designer's oversight, charging the client could damage the client-designer relationship andcause the loss of future business from that client. If the extra expense is a result of the client changing the requirements, then you need to fill out a revised estimate or change of work order or a new letter of agreement for the client to sign. Work order changes are so common in the construction industry that preprinted change orders are available at office supply stores. When the change order is written up, both the extra expenses and the extra completion time need to be clearly spelled out on paper.

PROJECT DELAYS

Late projects are very frustrating to both the client and the designer. Unavoidable delays occur frequently during design projects. Snow storms, for example, can delay deliveries and freight for several days. Accidents or illnesses to labor or workroom personnel can also cause delays. Whatever the cause of the delay, the designer should have an escape paragraph on his or her estimate and/or letter of agreement covering unavoidable delays. Never underestimate the time element in any design project; some clients will take the time you give them for a project very literally. Good continuous communication with the client reduces strife when delays on a project result from unforeseen events. It is a good idea to pad the schedule by a few days or a week—it is always better to look good for having a project come in early than to look bad for being late.

UNITED STATES AND METRIC SYSTEMS OF MEASURE

UNITED STATES SYSTEM

LINEAR

12 inches	=	1 foot
3 feet	=	1 yard
5½ yards	=	1 rod
40 rods	=	1 furlong
8 furlongs	=	1 mile (5,280 ft.)

SQUARE

144 sq. inches	=	1 sq. foot
9 sq. ft.	=	1 sq. yard
30¼ sq. yards	=	1 sq. rod
160 sq. rods	=	1 acre
640 acres	=	1 sq. mile

METRIC SYSTEM

LENGTH

1 kilometer	=	1,000 meters	=	3,280 feet, 10 inches
1 hectometer	=	100 meters	=	328 feet, 1 inch
1 meter	=	1 meter	=	39.37 inches
1 centimeter	=	.01 meter	=	.3937 inch
1 millimeter	=	.001 meter	=	.0394 inch
1 micron	=	.000001 meter	=	.000039 inch
1 millimicron	=	000000001 meter	=	.000000039 inch

SURFACE

1 sq. kilometer	=	1,000,000 sq. meters	=	.3861 sq. mile
1 hectare	=	10,000 sq. meters	=	2.47 acres
1 are	=	100 sq. meters	=	119.6 sq. yards
1 centare	=	1 sq. meter	=	1,550 sq. inches
1 sq. centimeter	=	.0001 sq. meter	=	.155 sq. inch
1 sq. millimeter	=	.000001 sq. meter	=	.00155 sq. inch

CARPET AREA TABLES
(Based on standard 9', 12', 15', & 18' widths)

SQUARE FOOT TABLE
Feet and Inches Converted to Square Feet

INCHES	9'	12'	15'	18'	INCHES	9'	12'	15'	18'
1	.75	1.00	1.25	1.50	7	5.25	7.00	8.75	10.50
2	1.50	2.00	2.50	3.00	8	6.00	8.00	10.00	12.00
3	2.25	3.00	3.75	4.50	9	6.75	9.00	11.25	13.50
4	3.00	4.00	5.00	6.00	10	7.50	10.00	12.50	15.00
5	3.75	5.00	6.25	7.50	11	8.25	11.00	13.75	16.50
6	4.50	6.00	7.50	9.00					

Feet	9'	12'	15'	18'	Feet	9'	12'	15'	18'
1	9.00	12.00	15.00	18.00	36	324.00	432.00	540.00	648.00
2	18.00	24.00	30.00	36.00	37	333.00	444.00	555.00	666.00
3	27.00	36.00	45.00	54.00	38	342.00	456.00	570.00	684.00
4	36.00	48.00	60.00	72.00	39	351.00	468.00	585.00	702.00
5	45.00	60.00	75.00	90.00	40	360.00	480.00	600.00	720.00
6	54.00	72.00	90.00	108.00					
7	63.00	84.00	106.00	126.00	41	369.00	492.00	615.00	700.00
8	72.00	96.00	120.00	144.00	42	378.00	504.00	630.00	756.00
9	81.00	108.00	135.00	162.00	43	387.00	516.00	645.00	774.00
10	90.00	120.00	150.00	180.00	44	396.00	528.00	660.00	792.00
					45	405.00	540.00	675.00	810.00
11	99.00	132.00	165.00	198.00	46	414.00	552.00	690.00	828.00
12	108.00	144.00	180.00	216.00	47	423.00	564.00	705.00	846.00
13	117.00	158.00	195.00	234.00	48	432.00	576.00	720.00	864.00
14	126.00	168.00	210.00	252.00	49	441.00	588.00	735.00	882.00
15	135.00	180.00	225.00	270.00	50	450.00	600.00	750.00	900.00
16	144.00	192.00	240.00	288.00					
17	153.00	204.00	255.00	306.00	51	459.00	612.00	765.00	918.00
18	162.00	216.00	270.00	324.00	52	468.00	624.00	780.00	936.00
19	171.00	228.00	285.00	342.00	53	477.00	636.00	795.00	954.00
20	180.00	240.00	300.00	360.00	54	486.00	648.00	810.00	972.00
					55	495.00	660.00	825.00	990.00
21	189.00	252.00	315.00	378.00	56	504.00	672.00	840.00	1008.00
22	198.00	264.00	330.00	396.00	57	513.00	684.00	855.00	1028.00
23	207.00	276.00	345.00	414.00	58	522.00	696.00	870.00	1044.00
24	216.00	288.00	360.00	432.00	59	531.00	708.00	885.00	1062.00
25	225.00	300.00	375.00	450.00	60	540.00	720.00	900.00	1080.00
26	234.00	312.00	390.00	468.00					
27	243.00	324.00	406.00	486.00	61	549.00	732.00	915.00	1098.00
28	252.00	336.00	420.00	504.00	62	558.00	744.00	930.00	1116.00
29	261.00	348.00	435.00	522.00	63	567.00	756.00	945.00	1134.00
30	270.00	360.00	450.00	540.00	64	576.00	768.00	960.00	1152.00
					65	585.00	780.00	975.00	1170.00
31	279.00	372.00	465.00	558.00	66	594.00	792.00	990.00	1188.00
32	288.00	384.00	480.00	576.00	67	603.00	804.00	1005.00	1206.00
33	297.00	396.00	495.00	594.00	68	612.00	816.00	1020.00	1224.00
34	306.00	408.00	510.00	612.00	69	621.00	828.00	1035.00	1242.00
35	315.00	420.00	525.00	630.00	70	630.00	840.00	1050.00	1260.00

Example—37' 7" of 12' width

37'	=	444 sq. ft
7"	=	7 sq. ft
Total	=	451 sq. ft

Bibliography

Allied Chemical Corporation. *Carpet College; Quality Analysis in Carpet, 1979 and Carpet Planning and Estimating, 1976.* Trenton, New Jersey: Allied Chemical Corporation, 1979

Allied Chemical Corporation. *Worry-free Guide to Buying Carpet.* Trenton: Allied Chemical Corporation, 1979.

Allied Chemical Corporation. *Smart Care for Carpet.* Allied Chemical Corporation. Trenton, New Jersey, 1976.

Allgaier, Al. *The Carpet Manual.* Cincinnati: Ralle Corporation, 1974.

Aronson, Joseph. *The Encyclopedia of Furniture.* New York: Crown Publications, Inc., 1965.

Art and History of Florence. Casa Editrice Bonechi, via Cairoli 18/b-50131 Firenze-Italia 1999

Better Homes & Gardens Baths. Des Moines: Meredith Corporation, 1996.

Better Homes & Gardens New Decorating Book. Des Moines: Meredith Corporation, 1981.

Duffin, D.J. *The Essentials of Modern Carpet Installation, 2nd Ed.* New York: Van Nostrand, 1962.

Faulknes, Ray and Sarah. *Inside Today's Home.* New York: Holt, Rinehart & Winston, 1975.

Helsel, Marjorie Borradaile. *The Interior Designer's Drapery,. Bedspread & Canopy Sketchfile.* New York: Whitney Library of Design, 1990.

Janson, H. W. *The History of Art.* New York: Prentice Hall/Abrams, 1969.

Lee, Sherman E. *A History of Far Eastern Art.* Prentice-Hall, Inc., Englewood Cliffs, N.J. and Harry N. Abrams, Inc. New York

O'Brien, M. *The Rug and Carpet Book.* New York: McGraw-Hill, 1951.

Philip, Peter. *Furniture of the World.* New York: Galahad, 1974.

Ramsey, L. G. C., ed. *The Complete Color Encyclopedia of Antiques.* London: Hawthorn Books, Inc., 1975.

Reznikoff, S.C. *Specifications For Commercial Interiors.* New York: Whitney Library of Design, 1989.

Rogers, Meyric R.. *American International Design.* New York: Bonanza Books, 1947.

Rupp, William with Friedmann, Arnold. *Construction Materials for Interior Design.* New York: Whitney Library of Design, 1989.

Siegel, Alan and Harry A. *Guide to Business Principles and Practices, Rev. Ed.* New York: Whitney Library of Design, 1982.

Sources & Design. Publisher; Naomi Anderson, Scottsdale, Az. 2000.

Spetty, Alexander. *The Styles of Ornament.* New York: Dover Publications, Inc., 1959.

Sunset Books. *Great Bathrooms.* Menlo Park: Sunset Books, 1999.

Sunset Books. *Ideas for Great Tile.* Menlo Park: Sunset Books 1998.

Sunset Magazine and Book Editors. *Curtains, Draperies & Shades.* Menlo Park: Sunset Books, 1979.

Treasures of Italy-Venice. *Civilization, Art and History.* Printed by Kina Italia S.p.A.- Milan 1999.

Whilton, Sherrill. *Interior Design & Decoration, 4th Ed.* Philadelphia: J. B. Lippincott Company, 1974.

Windows Beautiful. Sturgis. Michigan: Kirsh Publication, 1977, 1983, 1987.

Index